WM18

MCQs for the New MRCPsych Part 1

SPONSORED BY AN EDUCATIONAL GRANT FROM

MAKERS OF   SEROXAT
PAROXETINE

Other Examination Preparation Books Published by Petroc Press:

Balcombe	*Notes for the MRCP*	1900603470
Bateson	*Basic Tests in Gastroenterology*	1900603772
Bateson	*MCQs in Clinical Gastroenterology*	1900603519
Bateson	*MCQs on the Upper Digestive Tract*	1900603373
Bateson & Stephen	*MCQs in Gastroenterology*	1900603403
Black & Kelleher	*MCQs in Anaesthesiology*	1900603454
Chakravorty	*Visual Aids to the MRCP Examination*	0792388739
Chong & Wong	*Survival Kit for MRCP Part II*	1900603063
Edgell	*Preparing for MRCP Part II Cardiology*	0792388690
Green	*More MCQs for Finals*	079238928X
Green (Ed.)	*The MRCPsych Study Manual:* 2nd edn	1900603527
Helmy & Mokbel	*Preparing for the PLAB Part I*	1900603721
Hogston	*MCQs for the MRCoG Part II*	1900603551
Kazkaz *et al.*	*MCQs for the MCQs for the MRCP Part I*	1900603071
Kubba *et al.*	*MCQs for MFFP Part I*	1900603004
Levi	*Basic Notes in Psychiatry:* 2nd edn	1900603306
Levi	*Basic Notes in Psychotherapy*	1900603500
Levi	*Basic Notes in Psychopharmacology:* 2nd edn	1900603608
Levi	*MCQs in Psychiatry for MRCPsych*	1900603853
Levi	*PMPs for the MRCPsych Part II*	079238993X
Levi	*SAQs for the MRCPsych*	0746200994
Levy & Riordan Eva	*MCQs in Optics and Refraction*	1900603225
Levy & Riordan Eva	*MCQs for the FRCOphth*	1900603276
Levy & Riordan Eva	*MCQs for the MRCOphth*	1900603179
Mokbel	*MCQs in Applied Basic Medical Sciences*	1900603756
Mokbel	*MCQs in General Surgery*	1900603101
Mokbel	*MCQs in Neurology*	0792388577
Mokbel	*MCQs for the MRCS*	1900603829
Mokbel	*Operative Surgery and Surgical Topics for the FRCS/MRCS*	1900603705
Mokbel	*SAQs in Clinical Surgery-in-General for the FRCS*	190060390X
Ross & Emmanuel	*MCQs on Antimicrobial Therapy*	1900603411
Ross & Emmanuel	*MCQs in Medical Microbiology for MRCP*	0792388836
Ross & Emmanuel	*MCQs in Medical Microbiology and Infectious Diseases*	1900603365
Ross & Emmanuel	*MCQs in Microbiology and Infection for FRCS*	1900603152
Rymer & Higham	*Preparing for the DRCoG*	1900603012
Sandler & Sandler	*MCQs in Cardiology for MRCP Pt I*	0792389999
Sandler & Sandler	*MCQs in Cardiology*	0792389387
Sandler & Sandler	*More MCQs in Cardiology for MRCP Pt I*	0792388402
Sikdar	*MCQs in Basic Sciences for MRCPsych Pt II*	190060356X

Obtainable from all good booksellers or, in case of difficulty, from Plymbridge Distributors Limited, Plymbridge House, Estover Road, PLYMOUTH, Devon PL6 7PZ. Tel. 01752–202300; FAX 01752–202333

MCQs
for the
New MRCPsych Part 1

Michael Reilly, MB, BCh, BAO, MRCPsych
Clinical Research Fellow
St. Brigid's Hospital, Ballinasloe, Co. Galway, Ireland

and

Bangaru Raju, MD, MRCPsych, DPM
Consultant Psychiatrist
St. Mary's Hospital, Castlebar, Co. Mayo, Ireland

 PETROC PRESS

Petroc Press, an imprint of LibraPharm Limited

Distributors

Plymbridge Distributors Limited, Plymbridge House, Estover Road, Plymouth PL6 7PZ, UK

Copyright

©2001 LibraPharm Limited

While every attempt has been made to ensure that the information provided in this book is correct at the time of printing, the publisher, its distributors, sponsors and agents, make no representation, express or otherwise, with regard to the accuracy of the information contained herein and cannot accept any legal responsibility or liability for any errors or omissions that may have been made or for any loss or damage resulting from the use of the information.

First edition 2001
Reprinted 2001 (twice)

Published in the United Kingdom by
LibraPharm Limited
Gemini House
162 Craven Road
Newbury
Berkshire
RG14 5NR

A catalogue record for this book is available from the British Library

ISBN 1 900603 53 5

Printed and bound in the United Kingdom by
MPG Books Limited, Bodmin, Cornwall PL31 1EG

Dedication

We dedicate this book to our wives:

To Samantha and Prabha,
who have taught us more psychopathology
than any textbooks could have,
in the nicest possible ways!

Contents

Introduction

After employing an educational consultant to review the components of the membership examination, the Royal College of Psychiatrists decided to make a number of changes to both parts of the examination. Most parts of the examination were to be affected, both clinical and written, but, arguably, the changes likely to affect candidates most were the changes adopted to the multiple choices questions (MCQs) papers. The changes to the MCQ papers will be introduced into both parts of the MRCPsych examination, but the Part One MCQ paper will be the first to see the new format introduced. The main alterations to part one were to be phased in over a couple of sittings. These were:

1. Negative marking was abolished.
2. It became necessary to pass the MCQ paper to be allowed to progress to the clinical section of part one.
3. It was decided to change the format of the MCQ examination from 50 stem questions each with 5 items (250 total items to be answered) to 200 individual questions.
4. Assuming the pilots are successful, extended matching items (EMIs) will replace a certain proportion of the MCQs.
5. Criterion referenced marking will replace peer referenced marking.

At the time of writing the changes have progressed to the stage of (ii) above. Pilots of the EMIs have already been conducted along with the standard MCQ paper of the autumn 2000 Part One sitting. EMIs will be introduced into the examination assuming that analysis of the results of the EMIs show similar or better discrimination between candidates than that of the MCQs. At present however, the main changes to be introduced are those in (iii) above. The scrapping of the stem-and-items type questions was recommended so that many more topics could be broached in the course of the paper. The total number of items was reduced from 250 items to 200 items since more time will be involved in changing one's mindset from question to question in the new format examination.

This book was conceived as a response to this change of format for the MRCPsych Part One MCQ examination. While the basic format of 200 true or false questions is not completely different from the current format, most candidates prefer to have practised the components of the examination in as close a manner to reality as possible before the real thing. Timing is another issue: candidates will have to think more quickly on their feet since the potential to be examined on 200 unrelated topics is much more challenging than being examined on a mere 50 topics. A quick calculation shows that the candidate will now have just an average of 27 seconds to read, consider and answer a question in the 90-minute examination. We recommend strongly that any candidate using this book should attempt at least one of the papers under the strict time limit of the examination to become familiarised with the likely time pressure that will be encountered.

The composing of MCQs that are likely to be representative of the questions asked at the MRCPsych examination is always problematic. This is partly due to secretive way the College produces its MCQs and partly due to the changing nature of the MCQ examination. Recent years have seen a marked increase in the proportion of psychology MCQs asked at the expense of traditional part one areas such as psychopharmacology or psychopathology. The peer referenced system of marking appears to have necessitated moving away from areas where most candidates have prepared well to areas where it is more difficult to achieve sufficient knowledge in order to discriminate better between candidates. Peer referencing means that the examining board selects a certain centile as the pass mark (for the MRCPsych, this is usually about the 50th centile) with all candidates scoring this mark or above being successful. The disadvantage of this system is that if a good cohort of candidates sits the examination at a particular sitting, many will be penalised since only a fixed proportion (c. 50%) will pass. Criterion referenced marking will involve the examining board carefully scrutinising the paper and deciding what score a sufficiently prepared candidate would score on that paper. In the latter situation, theoretically 100% of candidates could pass the exam if all scored sufficiently high enough. This change in the marking system should help alleviate the traditional paranoid ideation among candidates sitting the examination that the College eagerly seeks their examination fees!

In writing this book we have the advantage of having been successful in both parts of the MRCPsych examination in relatively recent years. Our aim has been threefold. Firstly, to provide practice papers for the new format MRCPsych Part One MCQ paper. Secondly, to provide a more balanced mix of questions that corresponds more to the current paper make-up (note however that this is likely to be in vain, since even from the time we sat for part one the balance of questions has changed). Thirdly, and most importantly, we hope to provide an aid to studying for the MCQs. To this end we have attempted to set as many questions as we could on different aspects of the syllabus, focussing on areas we found to be either difficult or else of great relevance to the examination. The actual answers to individual MCQs are overall of peripheral interest: the main benefit in answering the MCQs is finding out where one's deficiencies in knowledge lie. If one is uncertain why a particular MCQ is true or false, one should try to look up the answer in whatever texts are available (the more the better).

It is difficult since the abolition of negative marking to give useful advice on the actual answering of questions, since the only sensible course is to answer all questions and to try to get as many correct as one possibly can. However we feel useful advice may be offered to candidates about how one can study for the MCQs. While we recognise that different methods of study suit different people, we feel that a couple of points we found useful in our preparations for the examination may be of benefit to some candidates, particularly those starting off:

(a) It is most useful to check the answers of MCQs from as many sources as possible and study according to your weaknesses as shown by your answers to the MCQs. This is the reverse of the intuitive course an individual may have of studying the material first and then seeing if one can answer related questions.

(b) The more people one has in a study group, the more efficiently can answers be tracked down in relevant sources. We consider 3–5 people an optimum number in a study group.

(c) While individual study is essential, individual study alone is considerably less efficient than group study for the MCQs.

(d) As many sources of MCQs as possible should be used. Textbooks of MCQs are useful to start off with and for individual study because they usually have answers and reasons for these answers listed. However they tend to make one lazy since one is less likely to look up relevant texts for answers of which one is unsure. In addition, the quality of MCQs in the textbooks varies greatly, from poor to a standard rarely achieved by professional examinations. Thus a candidate who has not seen MCQs that are double negatives, far too verbose, hopelessly ambivalent or downright wrong will be in for an unpleasant surprise on the day of the examination. It is thus essential to get as many of the poor-quality, dog-eared photocopies with coffee-mug stains of the MCQs that seem to hover about from examination to examination. While these usually have T's and F's scribbled beside them, the discussions about whether these are actually correct are most beneficial.

To assist candidates in using our MCQs to access textbooks to check material with which they find themselves unfamiliar, we have provided a reference list of the main texts we used while studying for the examination and in preparing these questions. Without exception, we would recommend all of the texts wholeheartedly to those studying for the MRCPsych. While it may not be essential for all candidates to have all of these books, a study group ought to have access to most of them. After each answer to an MCQ, we give a reference such as: **[D p356]**, which directs the reader to page 356 of the text listed as 'D' in the reference list. We recognise that many readers will find alternate references for questions that modify or refute the answers we have given; if anyone feels strongly about a particular question they may email comments to the following address: mcqs@ireland.com. Note however that it is a rare MCQ for which one can only find complete agreement in the literature about its answer.

Finally, while we hope this collection of MCQs will give candidates a better mix of topics that appear to be asked recently in the MRCPsych Part One, and that the format of the questions will help the candidate acclimatise to the changes due to the examination in autumn 2001, we realise that it is probably futile to try to produce a work that completely resembles the examination. This is mainly because while only a few authors are involved in writing an MCQ book, the Royal College of Psychiatrists makes use of many in writing MCQs, selecting appropriate questions from these and deciding the actual content or focus of the examination. Thus the MCQ papers are likely to remain changeable beasts that involve changing studying patterns over the years. Our main hope for our work is to provide a reasonable manner in which one can begin a campaign of study to candidates, particularly those who are just beginning to prepare for part one of the MRCPsych. If a number of people find this to be useful for them, then we will be satisfied that our goal has been achieved.

M.R.

Co. Galway, 2001 B.R.

Acknowledgements

While it is probably foolish to try to thank all who have assisted us with the preparation of this book in some shape or form, since we will undoubtedly forget and offend many, we cannot let the opportunity pass to express our appreciation to the following:

- Our colleagues and other staff in our workplaces for the numerous examples of support they have given us over the years. The encouragement, advice and feedback they have given us on this book have been invaluable. Particular thanks goes to Dr. Anne Jeffers who has been especially supportive of us both in training and in writing the book.
- We would like to thank the tutors of the Western Health Board Postgraduate Psychiatric Training Scheme, without whom we would not have got through our membership examinations.
- Our fellow trainees who have provided an excellent learning environment over the years and much interpersonal support.
- Our wives and families for their understanding of our frequent absences caused by studying (and now this book!).
- To Dhivya and Deepa for their tremendous help in the typing of questions.

Question Papers

Question Paper

Paper One

1.1 Bion suggested that his concept of the group basic assumption of 'pairing' was institutionalised in the aristocracy.

1.2 Only infants who are more than seven days old can imitate adult facial expressions.

1.3 Allport described five stages of discrimination, which included 'extermination'.

1.4 Two months old infants smile at the sight of their mother not because of conditions of rearing but due to an innate response.

1.5 A patient with anorexia nervosa who declares that 'if I put one pound, I'll end up putting on three stone' is demonstrating dichotomous reasoning.

1.6 William Blatz's security theory conceptualised that secured independence is not an impossible goal to achieve.

1.7 Children who display attachment behaviour of the disorganised-disorientated type in childhood tend to show preoccupied attachment behaviour as adults.

1.8 Theories like attractiveness, commonality and complementarity, which are proposed to explain mate selection, are not based on previous attachment experiences.

1.9 Janov is associated with the development of existential logo-therapy.

1.10 According to Parson's sick role, an illness needs to be legitimised by a medical professional in order for the individual to be exempted from normal social role responsibilities.

1.11 Patients with congenital agenesis of the corpus callosum, unlike individuals with acquired division of the callosum, tend to be able to feel an object with either hand and describe it verbally.

1.12 Kelly's fixed role therapy is not a simple procedure.

1.13 The construct repertory grid is a relatively useful tool to quantify traits of which the individual is both conscious and unconscious.

1.14 According to classical conditioning theory, parental drug abusing behaviour has the opposite unconditioned response to the conditioned response.

1.15 The cognitive theory of depression employs the idea of the cognitive triad of negative views of one's past, current situation and future.

1.16 'Ames room' experiments prove that an object's size remains constant no matter what its distance is from the observer.

1.17 In Klein's 'depressive position' the infant/child develops anxiety about its own safety, which leads to the characteristic thoughts and behaviours of this phase.

1.18 Main, Waters, Sroufe, Klaus and Grossmann are attachment theorists.

1.19 The term *narcissism* is used to describe the situation when an individual's libido is invested in the id.

1.20 In European countries, Hall's four zones of personal space are not clearly defined zones.

1.21 Groupthink tends to produce a balanced consideration of different possibilities because of the number of individuals involved.

1.22 Attachment theory is highly compatible with the 'general systems theory'.

1.23 Electromyographic activity in the muscles involved in speech production has been shown to be higher in patients with schizophrenia who are delusional as opposed to those who do not have delusions.

1.24 The Cannon-Bard theory of emotions does not explain the distress caused by a withdrawal reflex.

1.25 Eisenberg's five stages of pro-social reasoning development have empathic reasoning as the highest stage of development.

1.26 Social theorists call the gap between Western culture and the other cultures the 'cultural lag'.

1.27 Winnicott is associated with the term the 'pathological mother'.

1.28 Mechanic's illness behaviour always includes stages of recovery and rehabilitation.

1.29 Although most individuals recognise a piece a music more readily by listening to it with their left ear, a conductor is more likely to recognise music with his right ear.

1.30 The social skills model of Argyle is not based mainly on verbal feedback.

1.31 The Wechsler Adult Intelligent Scale – Revised (WAIS-R) generates three scaled scores.

1.32 According to Guilford, most intelligent tests do not test convergent thinking.

1.33 The phenomenon of cues suggests that the difficulties in memory in dementia may be more related to difficulty in retrieval rather than in storage of new material.

1.34 According to Sigmund Freud, the main energy source of cognitive functions is libido.

1.35 The membership examination of the Royal College of Psychiatrists is an example of a criterion-referenced test.

1.36 As the defence mechanism sublimation does not allow the direct expression of an impulse, on occasions it fails to be successful.

1.37 According to the Young-Helmholtz theory of colour vision, there are three types of receptors (cones) responsible for colour perception: short, medium and long receptors.

1.38 The experience of mood tends to be less intense than emotion.

1.39 Fixed interval reinforcement tends to produce a relatively constant rate of response from the subject.

1.40 Ego psychologist Heinz Hartmann emphasised 'competence' as opposed to 'drive reduction' as the major motivational factor.

1.41 Familiarisation with experiences or objects is disrupted by limbic and frontal lesions.

1.42 Psychoanalysts do not consider transference a form of unconscious resistance.

1.43 Piaget described how children who function in the concrete operational stage of development have developed the concept of ordinal numbers.

1.44 Bateson's marital skew relationship is a reciprocal relationship.

1.45 The Holmes and Rahe Social Readjustment Scale is an interviewer-rated scale used to rate life events for an individual.

1.46 Grief processes were first systematically studied by Murray Parkes.

1.47 According to Plutchik, the two primary emotions of acceptance and fear combine to give the secondary emotion of disappointment.

1.48 Among the five factors of Costa and McCrea, heritability is less for agreeableness than for conscientiousness.

1.49 Freud called his 'two principles of mental functioning' the primary and secondary processes.

1.50 Extraverts are less likely to abuse stimulant types of substances than the introverts are.

1.51 Hypnagogic states are associated with disturbances of body image.

1.52 In catalepsy, plastic resistance can sometimes be felt.

1.53 Flattening of affect in schizophrenia is often associated with anergia.

1.54 Parathymia is the indifference of schizophrenics to their own well-being.

1.55 Females with pseudocyesis may develop amenorrhoea and pigmentation of skin/nipples associated with pregnancy.

1.56 Verbigeration is a form of perseveration.

1.57 Normal leg movements may be shown while the patient is in bed, in those showing astasia abasia.

1.58 Phonemes are commonly found in schizophrenia.

1.59 Goldstein developed the idea of 'asyndesis' in his description of the reduction in logical connections apparent in the speech of patients with schizophrenia.

1.60 *Déjà entendu* can occur in focal occipital lobe epilepsy.

1.61 From the definition of the term 'neologism', a new word coined by a patient with schizophrenia is not a true neologism if one can easily see how the patient has derived the word.

1.62 During interviewing, facial expression and eye contact are the best indicators of malingering.

1.63 Panoramic recall is associated with temporal lobe disorder.

1.64 Memory can be reliably enhanced by hypnosis.

1.65 In chronic schizophrenia, age disorientation has been thought to correlate with intellectual impairment.

1.66 Malingering is also viewed as an arrest of development at an early age of life.

1.67 Somatopagnosia is synonymous with autopagnosia.

1.68 Pseudo-pseudodementia is a feature of retarded depression.

1.69 Derealisation is always an unpleasant experience to the individual.

1.70 Based on differential physiological changes, affect is divided into 'asthenic' and 'sthenic' types.

1.71 In advertence, when the interviewer speaks to the patient, the patient turns away in an exaggerated fashion from the interviewer.

1.72 Torpor and stupor can precede sopor.

1.73 Behaviour during automatism is often purposeless and inappropriate.

1.74 Alexithymia is a recognised feature of post-traumatic stress disorder.

1.75 Functional hallucinations occur when attention is focussed on a normal perception which is associated with the experience of the hallucination for the individual.

1.76 The rescaling of Holmes and Rahe's 'life change scale' since 1967 has shown a gradual rise in the values, but the original rankings remain constant.

1.77 Reed has described the thinking of those with anankastic personality traits as over-inclusive.

1.78 Dissimulation is deliberately concealing existing symptoms.

1.79 Benjamin Rush made one of the first classifications of phobias, describing such fears as that of death, ghosts and rum.

1.80 There is an elevated risk of death for bereaved women in the second year after bereavement.

1.81 An individual must make conscious effort to see the images in pareidolia.

1.82 Arthur Janov's concept of primal scream explains the symptoms of all mental disorders based on the 'sealing of emotions' during childhood.

1.83 Normal individuals will begin to hallucinate within a few hours of total sensory deprivation.

1.84 Obsessive thoughts are 'ego-alien'.

1.85 A prolonged sleep is a component of *mania à potu*.

1.86 Anna Freud did not describe the defence mechanism 'idealisation'.

1.87 Nerve conduction velocity studies have shown that there is an improvement in auditory perception in hyperacusis.

1.88 Proverb testing can be used to test formal thought disorder.

1.89 Patients occasionally describe a 'distinct' quality to hallucinatory perceptions, being able to distinguish them from real perceptions.

1.90 Carl Schneider's 'drivelling' thought disturbances are commonly found in paranoid schizophrenia.

1.91 In dreams, the individual retains the normal distinction between self and non-self.

1.92 Malapropisms are technical neologisms.

1.93 'Tram-line' thinking has been described as a component of Korsakoff's syndrome.

1.94 Phantom phenomena are only reported in somato-sensory systems.

1.95 The alternation between opposite movements that can occur in catatonic schizophrenia is known as ambivalence.

1.96 In amnesia following a crime, the presence of amnesia for an appreciable period of time prior to the criminal act is crucial to be certain about true amnesia.

1.97 The term *Gedankenlautwerden* is synonymous with the term *echo de pensées*.

1.98 Bleuler's 'four A's' are found in type II schizophrenia only.

1.99 Particular types of perseveration are palilalia and logoclonia.

1.100 Jung's 'persona' can be compared to Winnicott's 'false self'.

1.101 Clozapine levels may be increased when co-administered with fluvoxamine since the latter inhibits the cytochrome P450 enzyme 2D6.

1.102 With increasing doses, fluoxetine shows non-linear pharmacokinetics.

1.103 Phenelzine is associated with pyridoxine deficiency.

1.104 Normalisation of previously abnormal dexamethasone suppression test or TRH stimulation test may indicate that a patient can safely discontinue antidepressant drug treatment.

1.105 During the third trimester of pregnancy, it may be necessary to reduce the dose of methadone maintenance for a dependent patient since methadone metabolism tends to decrease then.

1.106 SSRIs are not effective in depression that is resistant to treatment with more conventional antidepressants.

1.107 Because of their pharmacokinetics, anticholinergic drugs tend to be poorly absorbed from the gastrointestinal tract.

1.108 Tertiary amines such as amitriptyline are more potent at α_2-receptor sites than the secondary amines (e.g. nortriptyline), or phentolamine (an α-adrenoreceptor antagonist).

1.109 Carbamazepine has 70% to 80% plasma protein binding.

1.110 A divided daily dosage schedule of lithium is safer for the kidney than once daily administration as the former will give more plateau-like blood levels over 24 hours whereas the later will produce high serum peak levels followed by a marked trough.

1.111 Topiramate tends to lower serum concentrations of carbamazepine when co-administered.

1.112 Vinegar, commercial yoghurt, dairy cheese, cream cheese, octopus and sausages can be consumed safely by patients who are on monoamine oxidase inhibitors.

1.113 Since it is a $5HT_2$ receptor antagonist, mirtazepine has reduced nausea in its side-effect profile when compared to the SSRIs.

1.114 When compared to per oral administration, rectal administration of drugs does not cause a significant difference in first pass metabolism.

1.115 Brewed tea contains less caffeine than brewed coffee.

1.116 When clozapine is stopped at the onset of leucopenia before agranulocytosis develops, the risk of progression to agranulocytosis is certainly prevented.

1.117 Citalopram does not inhibit the cytochrome P450 2D6 isoenzyme.

1.118 When compared to fluvoxamine, fluoxetine is present in larger amounts in breast milk.

1.119 The only antidepressant with a known therapeutic window is desipramine.

1.120 Chlorpromazine can be safely given to patients with myasthenia gravis.

1.121 Loxapine inhibits noradrenaline reuptake from the synaptic cleft.

1.122 Amantadine is unlikely to improve antipsychotic drug-induced tremors.

1.123 Lithium is found to be an effective treatment in only 40–50% of patients who receive it.

1.124 A higher risk of movement disorders with trimipramine and clomipramine has been reported as they have more affinity for dopamine (D_2) receptors when compared to amitriptyline.

1.125 In animals, a single dose of phenothiazines has been shown to lead to a rapid (within 12 hours) decrease in dopaminergic activity.

1.126 Digoxin may impair the clinical effect of lithium.

1.127 Serotonin-dopamine antagonists block the normal inhibitory effects that serotonin has on dopaminergic neurons in the meso-cortical pathway by antagonising the $5HT_{1A}$ heteroreceptor on dopaminergic neurons.

1.128 During lactation, the use of three neuroleptics (clozapine, pimozide and sulpiride) is mainly singled out for special caution.

1.129 Neuroleptic malignant syndrome is twice as common in males as in females.

1.130 In high serum levels, sodium valproate can cause cerebellar signs.

1.131 When given to rodents, dopamine receptor antagonists cause a syndrome of abnormal posturing and increased spontaneous motor activity.

1.132 Butyrophenones (e.g. haloperidol) block sigma opioid receptors but lack morphine like activity.

1.133 Pindolol may augment the action of the selective serotonin reuptake inhibitors by blocking postsynaptic $5HT_{1A}$ receptors.

1.134 The clinical potency of antipsychotics does not correlate with noradrenaline blocking effects.

1.135 Anandamide is a lipid neurotransmitter that is thought be a natural analogue of tetrahydrocannabinol.

1.136 Unrealistic expectations of treatment by the patient and the unrealistic belief that they are being deprived of something that would benefit them are forms of nocebo effect.

1.137 Milnacipran is a selective serotonin-noradrenaline reuptake inhibitor that has been reported to have a faster onset of anti-depressant action than conventional antidepressants.

1.138 The maximal psychomotor impairment and the recovery time from it are more marked with oxazepam than with diazepam.

1.139 The emergence of sustained hypertension with venlafaxine is dose-related.

1.140 Gastrointestinal symptoms such as vomiting and diarrhoea are common adverse effects of valproate.

1.141 In double-blinded drug trials comparing antidepressants with placebo, it is quite rare for patients shown eventually to have received placebo to complain of dry mouth, thus creating difficulty with the blinding technique.

1.142 When the size of a tablet is bigger, the placebo effect is more pronounced.

1.143 Dopamine antagonism in the mesocortical pathway is thought to contribute to the formation of secondary negative symptoms in schizophrenia.

1.144 Postural hypotension and tachycardia are reported with selective serotonin reuptake inhibitors.

1.145 Buspirone binds to dopamine D_2 receptors in the central nervous system.

1.146 Hydroxylation of tricyclic tertiary amine antidepressants, e.g. imipramine, is the rate-limiting step in their metabolism and this converts tertiary compounds to secondary amines that are also active compounds.

1.147 Up to 20% of many dopamine receptor antagonists are excreted unchanged in the urine.

1.148 With antipsychotics, the risk of developing acute dystonia is positively associated with age.

1.149 The retinal pigmentation that may be produced by treatment with thioridazine may progress even after the drug has been stopped.

1.150 None of the SSRIs alter the half-life of diazepam.

1.151 Meduna was one of the first to use ECT (electroconvulsive therapy) therapeutically.

1.152 According to DSM-IV, sexual symptoms are a recognised feature but they need not be present to make a diagnosis of somatisation disorder.

1.153 Around 70% of patients with schizophrenia have at least one Schneiderian first rank symptom.

1.154 The commonest cause of delirium in the elderly is vascular pathology.

1.155 DSM-IV mirrors the ICD-10 convention of classifying obsessive-compulsive disorders and anxiety disorders separately in the classification.

1.156 Claustrophobia, a type of specific phobia, commonly manifests in the early twenties.

1.157 The association between agoraphobia and mitral valve prolapse has not been consistently replicated.

1.158 Children who start cross-dressing early are more likely to become transvestites.

1.159 Premenstrual syndrome is associated with increased risk of thyroid dysfunction.

1.160 Decreased levels of dopamine are thought to be responsible for depressed mood in alcohol withdrawal and over-activity in delirium tremens.

1.161 Decreased total REM sleep has been described in bereaved individuals.

1.162 In the primary prevention of drug abuse, resistance strategies are more successful than providing alternative facilities to drug use.

1.163 Sisters of patients with anorexia nervosa have a risk of approximately 7% of developing this condition.

1.164 Alcohol withdrawal fits do not occur after fifth day following abstinence.

1.165 In contrast with other forms of depression, seasonal affective disorder is commoner in males.

1.166 Anxiety responses in the Rorschach test are heightened colour responses, animal movement responses and unstructured form responses.

1.167 About 15% of patients with bipolar affective disorder start off their course of illness with three consecutive depressive episodes.

1.168 Difficulty in estimating time is a recognised feature of parietal lobe lesions.

1.169 Depression that occurs for the first time in the elderly is associated with higher risk of recurrence than is depression that occurs earlier in life.

1.170 Complex partial seizure is an alternative term for temporal lobe epilepsy.

1.171 Around 40% of patients with dementia have either auditory or visual hallucinations at some stage during the illness.

1.172 Morbidly jealous women are typically younger than morbidly jealous men.

1.173 Ferenczi was one of the first to apply psychoanalytical theory to theories of disease pathogenesis by suggesting conversion processes could work on the autonomic nervous system.

1.174 In International Classification of Diseases and Related Health Problems (ICD-10), 'ego-dystonic homosexuality' has been listed as a diagnostic category.

1.175 Group psychotherapeutical approaches have been shown to produce increases in natural killer (NK) cell numbers and activity in cancer patients.

1.176 Morphometric magnetic resonance imaging in obsessive-compulsive disorder does not show structural abnormalities of the brain.

1.177 A recent study has confirmed the usefulness of the Hamilton cuff technique to monitor seizures during ECT.

1.178 Sadism and masochism are often exclusive perversions and rarely present as preferential perversions.

1.179 About a third of women who develop puerperal psychosis have been previously admitted to a psychiatric hospital.

1.180 Schizotypal personality disorder is characterised by unusual personal experiences, eccentric behaviour, suspiciousness and detached behaviour.

1.181 Patients with schizoaffective disorder tend to have the same mixture of positive and negative symptoms that patients with schizophrenia have, but with an overlay of affective symptoms.

1.182 Prange's permissive biogenic amine hypothesis states that a serotonin deficit permits the expression of mania.

1.183 Elevated or irritable mood must be present for at least a week for a hypomanic episode to be diagnosed using DSM-IV.

1.184 Major depressive disorder is more common in blacks than in whites.

1.185 Lower levels of harm avoidance are associated with lower levels of plasma GABA.

1.186 Henry Maudsley coined the term 'affective disorder'.

1.187 The proportion of psychiatric patients who have a personality disorder is in the region of a quarter of all patients.

1.188 Tension, nausea and headache are more common in panic disorder than in generalised anxiety disorder.

1.189 Panic disorder is probably less common among the elderly than it is among young adults.

1.190 The majority of cases of early onset dementia of the Alzheimer's type have been suggested to be linked to a mutation on chromosome 14 designated S182.

1.191 In Great Britain about half of elderly patients in residential care have dementia.

1.192 Frontal lobe seizures can reliably be differentiated from non-epileptic seizures, by demonstrating an elevated serum prolactin immediately following a seizure attack.

1.193 Eating disorders are almost twice as common in adolescent females with type 1 diabetes as in their non-diabetic peers.

1.194 The national co-morbidity survey showed that race, ethnicity and living in an urban environment predicted a lifetime history of drug dependence.

1.195 One study showed that the mortality from electroconvulsive therapy was significantly lower than that of psychotherapy over a three-year period.

1.196 The neurodevelopmental hypothesis does not account for neuro-physiological impairments in schizophrenia.

1.197 Parsons described factitious disorders as being at one end of the spectrum of the sick role.

1.198 Schizoaffective disorder can be viewed as a condition occupying an intermediate position in a continuum of a single psychosis, schizophrenia at one end and mood disorders at the other end.

1.199 Depersonalisation has been associated with haloperidol treatment.

1.200 Avoidant personality disorder is more prevalent than anankastic personality disorder.

Paper Two

2.1 The term *countercathexis* is sometimes used in psychoanalysis to refer to the resistance to remembering.

2.2 According to Piaget, 'conservation of weight' is achieved at the age of six.

2.3 Dream work involves condensation, displacement and symbolic repression.

2.4 Increasing the brightness of the television screen will slow down our perception of it.

2.5 The fundamental attribution error suggests that we have a schema of cause and effect for human behaviour that gives too much weight to the situation and not enough to the person.

2.6 The original 'Thematic Apperception Test' (TAT), developed by Murray and Morgan consists of a set of 20 pictures.

2.7 Franz Alexander applied psychodynamic theory to seven particular medical illnesses in developing a psychosomatic approach to medicine.

2.8 Margaret Mahler's separation-individuation phase consists of 'differentiation, practising, emotional object constancy and *rapprochement* and individuality' sub-phases.

2.9 According to Alfred Adler, lack of social interest in an individual indicated that the individual had gained a 'sense of mastery' and no longer felt the same need for competition.

2.10 Research findings suggest that perinatal death of a child may result in more intense grief than an unexpected infant death.

2.11 In classical conditioning, incubation refers to repeated brief exposures to a stimulus, leading to an increase in the strength of the conditioned response.

2.12 Type A traits show a distinct single uniform behaviour pattern.

2.13 A Thurstone scale uses five points to distinguish level of agreement with a presented statement.

2.14 *Laissez-faire* leadership is not suitable for creative, group-oriented tasks.

2.15 Broadbent's 'early selection' theory of selective attention suggests that while all sensory data is fully processed, only a certain amount is selected in choosing an appropriate reaction.

2.16 Studies of adult attachment behaviour have showed that among Grice's four co-operative principles of coherent conversation, the quality of maxim was the most important.

2.17 The congruity theory of Osgood and Tannenbaum holds that when an individual develops two beliefs that are incompatible, both of the beliefs tend to change.

2.18 Wildavsky thought that 'deinstitutionalisation' and 'demedicalisation' did not occur in the interest of patients.

2.19 Freud considered infantile sexuality to have one main source of sexual excitation.

2.20 According to the negative-state relief model of Cialdini, people tend to try to escape from situations where they feel intolerable anxiety as soon as it is possible.

2.21 Chomsky's theory of an innate 'language acquisition device' suggests that language development is dependent on other non-linguistic cognitive processes being intact.

2.22 Herbert Simon was awarded the Nobel prize for his theories of psychological processes based on computer-simulated experiments.

2.23 Attempts have been made to explain the high incidence of agoraphobia in young married women in terms of the concept of 'role rejection'.

2.24 Affectional bonds are long lasting and dyadic in nature.

2.25 The relative ease that one can condition an individual to have a phobia of animals as opposed to a packet of cigarettes is an example of 'preparedness'.

2.26 The Bielefeld longitudinal study of attachment behaviour did not find a longitudinal relationship between early attachment quality to the mother or father and perceived parental support for the child.

2.27 In Piaget's pre-operational stage, children develop the concept of 'reversibility'.

2.28 Freud's 'dual theory of drives' rejects the equal involvement of sexual and aggressive drives in motivating behaviour.

2.29 Sounds that gradually increase in loudness are more difficult to localise than sounds with sudden onset.

2.30 The intelligence test 'Raven's Progressive Matrices' comes in three versions.

2.31 Karen Horney saw 'alienation from self' as one of the major processes in the occurrence of psychosis in her psychodynamic theory.

2.32 There is significant evidence to support Winch's theory of complementarity that a dominant partner paired with a submissive one produces a good relationship.

2.33 Approximately half of schizophrenic patients show abnormalities on span-of-attention tests.

2.34 Fairburn thought that the libidinal attitude determines the object relationship.

2.35 The correlation of intelligence quotient (IQ) score for identical twins reared apart is approximately 0.85, from familial studies of intelligence.

2.36 Suddenness and transferability are the characteristics of 'trial and error' learning.

2.37 The pressure for conformity in a group diminishes if the group is not unanimous.

2.38 Bowlby felt that a child is not capable of goal-corrected partnership until the child is aged six.

2.39 The general physiological response to stress according to Seyle includes exhaustion.

2.40 Persistent negligence and abuse by an attachment figure will gradually diminish the attachment.

2.41 Observing another person perform a decision making task has been shown to help a subject's subsequent performance of the task, even if the processes necessary for the task's completion are not readily evident.

2.42 Foucault strongly argued for the 'anti-psychiatry' school.

2.43 The gradual withdrawal of prompts used to guide an individual to a desired response after the response has become well established to known as 'abolishing'.

2.44 Lorenz wrote about his imprinting theory in his famous book *King Solomon's Ring*.

2.45 In the 10-year follow-up to the Black Report, Smith *et al.* (1990) found that differences in the mortalities of the social classes had widened.

2.46 The short-term memory has a capacity of seven letters or three chunks.

2.47 Festinger's cognitive dissonance is a form of extrinsic motivation theory.

2.48 According to Asch, in a small group the presence of one racially different dissenter on a neutral subject could reduce the conformity rate among other individuals who belong to a common different racial origin.

2.49 Gestalt psychology describes the perceptual phenomenon of the law of unity.

2.50 According to attachment theory, those who have compulsive self-reliance bonding do not show abnormal grief.

2.51 Somnambulism occurs more frequently in children and in females.

2.52 Echo behaviour can be based on the memory image of another person.

2.53 The palimpsest is a common symptom of early alcohol dependence.

2.54 Rapt intense looking and over-activity without interfering are the characteristic features of ecstatic states.

2.55 A gross disorder of basic drives has been described as one of the characteristics of psychotic states.

2.56 Sleeping less than 75% of the normal amount for one's age is considered abnormal.

2.57 Leonhard divided his categories of 'cycloid psychoses' into three subdivisions: anxiety-happiness, confusion and amotivational psychosis.

2.58 According to Meninger, hostility in suicide has three components: a 'wish to kill', a 'wish to be killed' and a 'wish to die'.

2.59 Jasper's (1913) definition of 'pseudohallucinations' included the idea that they are vivid mental images, occurring in internal space and are changeable by an effort of will.

2.60 Eugen Bleuler's fundamental symptoms include disturbance of the subjective experience of self.

2.61 Mitgehen is a form of mitmachen.

2.62 According to Munro, monosymptomatic hypochondriacal psychosis can be characterised either by delusion of halitosis or delusions of the dysmorphic type or delusional infestation.

2.63 The actual meaning of 'anaclitic' is 'without a carer'.

2.64 The psychodynamic theory of Bibring describes aggression in depression as an expression of conflicts within the ego.

2.65 The term 'apophany' has been used occasionally to denote a secondary delusional experience.

2.66 Dysmegalopsia caused by weakened accommodation but normal convergence is similar to the dysmegalopsia caused by papilloedema.

2.67 Forgetting of information that is actually being repressed because of associated painful affect has been termed 'anathymic amnesia'.

2.68 In fugue states, there is no restriction in the level of consciousness.

2.69 Memory deficits in schizophrenia have been reported to involve mainly semantic memory.

2.70 In *Wahnstimmung* the first change is in ideas, which leads on to perplexed mood.

2.71 Ganser described his eponymous syndrome in 1898 after observing 104 criminals with varying degrees of the constituent symptoms.

2.72 Social therapy mostly employs Rapoport's principles of communalism, democracy, permissiveness and reality confrontation.

2.73 The auditory hallucinations that occur in acute organic states are usually elementary hallucinations.

2.74 Double orientation is a term used at times to describe multiple personality.

2.75 When asked to estimate the length of time the interview with their doctor lasted, patients with schizophrenia of the non-paranoid types tend to underestimate the time more than patients with paranoid schizophrenia.

2.76 Neuro-linguistic programming practitioners mainly use hypnotic procedures.

2.77 Patients with amnesia resulting from hippocampal lesions tend to deny their memory difficulties.

2.78 In *déjà vu* phenomena, misidentification will never occur.

2.79 Dysmegalopsia describes a change in the quality of perceptions where objects are seen as being uniformly larger than their real size.

2.80 Gender interchangeability after the age of five, in order to establish the correct genetic sex, is invariably impossible.

2.81 Lack of substantiality does not distinguish pseudohallucinations from hallucinations.

2.82 *Wurgstimme* is a disorder of the flow of speech.

2.83 Schneider considered personality disorders and neuroses to be qualitatively different from normal experiences or traits.

2.84 Black patch disease is a psychosis due to an under-stimulated state.

2.85 Cataplexy, the inordinate maintenance of postures or physical attitudes, is seen most often associated with catatonic schizophrenia.

2.86 In receptive aphasia, the patient's speech is irrelevant and incoherent.

2.87 A patient who experiences a loss of awareness of time, feeling that time has been removed, is experiencing a form of passivity.

2.88 Rapport will be more difficult to establish with a delirious patient, if one speaks loudly.

2.89 It is not possible to understand how a patient with schizophrenia has derived a neologism.

2.90 A person's failing to see his own image in a mirror is an example of a nihilistic delusion.

2.91 Unsystematised delusions are more commonly seen in those who develop schizophrenia later on in life as opposed to those who develop it earlier in life.

2.92 Eidetic imagery may be pathological.

2.93 Clinical vampirism in a patient is usually related to a diagnosis of schizophrenia.

2.94 Asyndesis results in speech incoherence.

2.95 Tyrer considers irritability to be a separate mood state from that of anxiety.

2.96 In Cawley's classification, the fourth and final type of psychotherapy is behavioural therapies.

2.97 One of the commonest forms of hypnagogic auditory hallucination is the experience of hearing one's own name spoken aloud.

2.98 During adolescence, erratic work patterns and inconsistent and paradoxical behaviour indicate minimal psychopathology.

2.99 In disorders of thought, 'Knight's move' thinking has also been described as 'dereistic' thinking.

2.100 Cloninger's dimensions of personality such as reward seeking, harm avoidance and persistence are based on operant conditioning principles.

2.101 Increased serotinergic transmission to the hypothalamus is thought to be one of the mechanisms whereby the selective serotonin reuptake inhibitors improve symptoms in panic disorder.

2.102 Thioridazine and chlorpromazine cause mydriasis.

2.103 The fatal hepatotoxicity associated with sodium valproate occurs mainly in patients on high-dose regimens.

2.104 Flupenthixol can be safely used in pregnancy.

2.105 The antihistamine diphenhydramine has been used for the treatment of extrapyramidal side-effects.

2.106 Decreased concentration of endozepines, the endogenous ligands with benzodiazepine receptor agonist effects, have been found in the cerebrospinal fluid of patients with panic disorder.

2.107 Buspirone is almost entirely excreted in the urine, following metabolism.

2.108 Two dosage forms of the same drug (e.g. regular preparation and slow release preparation) with an equal bioavailability are bioequivalent.

2.109 Akathisia and Parkinsonism have been reported with diltiazem.

2.110 Midazolam does not impair memory function as it has a short half-life (1–2 hours).

2.111 Risperidone is a member of the benzisoxazole antipsychotic drugs class.

2.112 The concentration of trazodone in the brain is higher than its plasma concentration and its plasma protein binding capacity.

2.113 Citalopram has no proconvulsive effect.

2.114 During treatment, fluoxetine can produce both hypoglycaemia and hyperglycaemia.

2.115 Zolpidem has a half-life of about 5 hours.

2.116 Amiloride diuretics are the drugs of choice to control polyuria induced by lithium.

2.117 Lithium reduces libido in significant numbers of patients.

2.118 The uptake of a drug by the liver and subsequent renal tubular secretion are important factors in drugs that obey zero-order kinetics.

2.119 Ziprasidone is associated with marked weight gain.

2.120 Clomipramine is probably more effective in obsessive-compulsive disorder than SSRIs.

2.121 Amoxapine is a tricyclic antidepressant with dopamine blocking activity and high anticholinergic activity.

2.122 Benzodiazepines do not interfere with recall of old information acquired before the initiation of benzodiazepine treatment.

2.123 Clonidine may be used for the treatment of affective disorders.

2.124 Benzodiazepines can induce mania.

2.125 Zolpidem has hypnotic and muscle-relaxant properties.

2.126 Antipsychotics are reversibly and adynamically bound to peripheral sites that have a rich blood supply.

2.127 Tetrabenazine acts by depleting catecholamines stored pre-synaptically, and has been used in the treatment of tardive dyskinesia.

2.128 Propranolol can increase plasma levels of thyroxine.

2.129 Phenylcyclidine has antagonist activity at NMDA glutamate receptors.

2.130 The risk of side-effects is minimised if total plasma levels of tricyclic antidepressants are lower than 300 ng/ml.

2.131 Reserpine produces its antipsychotic effects by blockade of mainly dopamine D_2 and D_3 receptors.

2.132 Antidepressants can have anticonvulsant effects upon ECT.

2.133 The half-life of sertindole is 20 hours.

2.134 Trazodone has less effect on noradrenaline re-uptake blockade than clomipramine.

2.135 Loxapine is one of the antipsychotic agents least associated with weight gain in patients.

2.136 Amoxapine does not have active metabolites.

2.137 The efficacy of propranolol for the treatment of akathisia has not been proven by any studies to date.

2.138 In an epileptic patient with schizophrenia, at therapeutic doses loxapine has a lower risk than clozapine to adversely effect epileptic control.

2.139 Fluoxetine taken by a pregnant mother is associated with perinatal complications especially if it is taken in the third trimester.

2.140 T wave inversion on the ECG is not an uncommon non-toxic side-effect of lithium.

2.141 Drinking grapefruit juice repeatedly increases the half-life of triazolam by approximately 50% via CYP3A4 inhibition.

2.142 In short-term benzodiazepine treatment, due to its half-life, diazepam has a relatively long duration of action.

2.143 Drowsiness associated with conventional antipsychotics is largely a result of their α_1-antagonism.

2.144 In higher doses, venlafaxine has an increased risk of hypotension.

2.145 After one year of treatment about 5% of patients receiving antipsychotic medication will have developed tardive dyskinesia.

2.146 The therapeutic index is the ratio of maximum effective concentration and the minimum tolerated concentration.

2.147 Sertraline may be found in significant amounts in the breast milk of lactating females.

2.148 Lithium can cause non-toxic goitre, hypothyroidism, hyperthyroidism, and elevations of parathormone and serum calcium.

2.149 Intravenous barbiturates are useful in performing the Wada test.

2.150 The re-uptake blockade of amine neurotransmitters does not bear any relationship to the onset of clinical efficacy of antidepressants.

2.151 Patients with puerperal mania have similar numbers of first-degree relatives with mania as have patients with mania not associated with pregnancy/delivery.

2.152 Dysthymic disorder frequently co-exists with borderline personality disorder.

2.153 After the fenfluramine challenge test, patients with bulimia nervosa who are of normal weight tend to show a decreased prolactin response.

2.154 The Epidemiological Catchment Area study reported a high prevalence of depression in those who were co-habitant.

2.155 In individuals with coronary artery disease, the prevalence of depressive disorders is higher in men than in women.

2.156 Delusional ideas in depression are commonly persecutory in nature.

2.157 The diagnosis of schizoid personality disorder is made more commonly in males.

2.158 DSM-IV has carefully avoided cultural consideration in the diagnostic discussion of schizophrenia and other mental disorders to maximise its use in other parts of the world.

2.159 In depression, REM latency is reduced from 90 minutes to about 40 minutes.

2.160 ICD-10 classifies all disorders which result from reactions to stresses under one category.

2.161 Approximately 30% of outpatients on long-term antipsychotic treatment develop Parkinsonism.

2.162 Blushing is characteristic of social phobia, schizotypal personality disorder and avoidant personality disorder.

2.163 First rank symptoms are rare in late onset schizophrenia.

2.164 HIV dementia is not reported during the (physically) asymptomatic or immunocompetent phase.

2.165 In trichotillomania the plucking of hairs from areas apart from the scalp is rare.

2.166 Adrenocorticotropic hormone response to corticotrophin-releasing hormone is blunted in anorexia nervosa, bulimia nervosa and weight loss.

2.167 Estimates suggest that the prevalence of personality disorders in the general population is at least 10%.

2.168 Intoxication of dexamphetamine, magic mushroom, methadone and morning glory seeds cause mydriasis.

2.169 Recent studies have shown that the traditional seasonal variations in suicide rates have become more accentuated over the past 20 years.

2.170 β-amyloid deposition and hyperphosphorylated tau protein are not specific to dementia of the Alzheimer type.

2.171 Comorbid alcohol abuse is more common in social phobia than in the other phobias.

2.172 Patients with dementia secondary to non-metastatic manifestations of carcinoma invariably show normal brain scans.

2.173 Electroconvulsive therapy has been shown by a number of studies to be effective for the treatment of the negative symptoms of schizophrenia, but its use is limited by the difficulties in its chronic administration.

2.174 There is definite proof that risk of developing delirium tremens begins at consumption of twelve units of alcohol per day.

2.175 Almost all studies investigating the effects of reducing type A behaviour on coronary events have shown little or no benefits.

2.176 The St. Louis (Feigner) criteria for schizophrenia identify patients who are difficult to treat.

2.177 Many studies have shown outcome for elderly depressed patients to be at least as good as, or better than, that for younger depressed patients.

2.178 Situationally predisposed panic attacks invariably occur on exposure to or in anticipation of that situation.

2.179 Hypomanic episodes typically have a gradual onset.

2.180 Fear of crowds indicates agoraphobia.

2.181 Patients with bulimia nervosa who binge frequently have significantly lower CSF 5-HIAA concentrations than normal controls do.

2.182 Increased sexual drive in depression always indicates a mixed state.

2.183 The presence of perplexity in an individual with schizophrenia predicts a poor response to electroconvulsive therapy.

2.184 Hypofrontality in schizophrenia has been demonstrated both during prefrontal functional activities and non-prefrontal functional activities.

2.185 Misidentification phenomena occurring in Alzheimer's disease tend to occur in older rather than younger patients.

2.186 The commonest psychiatric morbidities during alcohol withdrawal states are anxiety and depressive disorders.

2.187 Children of parents who develop post-traumatic stress disorder have been shown to have lower levels of cortisol than children of 'normal' parents.

2.188 Opioid abusers commonly accept family members' involvement in their rehabilitation.

2.189 There is an increased risk of dissocial personality disorder in the relatives of male probands with this disorder than there is in the relatives of female probands.

2.190 In sex addiction, paraphilias are invariable.

2.191 Melancholic depressed mood is often described by patients as being qualitatively different from normal sad mood.

2.192 Da Costa's syndrome may be associated with hypochondriacal delusions.

2.193 Isolated panic attacks occur in about 15% of the general population at some stage over their lives.

2.194 William Gull first described anorexia nervosa.

2.195 Social phobia has consistently been shown to be more prevalent in males.

2.196 According to DSM-IV the symptoms of adjustment disorder are maladaptive and occur in reaction to significant stressors.

2.197 The differential diagnosis of fibromyalgia includes somatization disorder.

2.198 Alzheimer's disease and Lewy body dementia do not have a common genetic risk factor.

2.199 Third ventricle tumours are associated with manic episodes.

2.200 Depression is more common in Cushing's disease due to pituitary pathology than in Cushing's syndrome secondary to corticosteroid therapy.

Paper Three

3.1 In Runciman's 'relative deprivation' theory of prejudice, fraternal deprivation refers to an individual feeling that his brothers are treating him unfairly.

3.2 According to psychoanalytical theory, fixation in the anal stage can lead to messy, disorderly, disorganised, careless and extravagant behaviour.

3.3 Individuals who are members of a majority group tend to see the members of their own group as being more homogenous than people who are members of a different group.

3.4 Hooley and Teasdale found that among expressed emotions, a highly critical attitude of the spouse predicted relapse of depressive disorder.

3.5 Winnicott is associated with the terms integration and personalisation.

3.6 Disposition personality research is focused on personality characteristics that can be assessed over time to demonstrate intra-individual variability and inter-individual stability between members of species.

3.7 Freud was the author of the book *Project for a Scientific Psychology*.

3.8 Kavanagh felt that a high level of an expressed emotion in a person could be viewed as that person's enduring character.

3.9 Piaget stated that children functioning at the concrete operational stage lack a logic of class hierarchy.

3.10 Olson's 'circumplex model' of family function has described sixteen possible types of family systems, which are based only on cohesion and adaptability dimensions.

3.11 If the word 'select' is read as 'object' by the patient, one should suspect the presence of a neglect dyslexia.

3.12 Galen termed hot-tempered personality as phlegmatic and apathetic personality as choleric.

3.13 For C. G. Jung the 'shadow' refers to the part of the ego that contains only the negative traits of the individual.

3.14 According to Weston's five levels of object relations, persons at level 3 are more likely to develop personality disorder.

3.15 The notion of the 'schizophrenogenic mother' was expounded by Fromm-Reichman.

3.16 When the Thematic Apperception Test is administered twice to the same subject, the themes of the two different stories given by the individual to the same cards are typically similar.

3.17 Love is a primary emotion according to Plutchik.

3.18 Baumeister and Leary's theory of 'belongingness as a fundamental need' states that people often wish to have several close affiliations.

3.19 Erikson's stage of 'initiative vs. guilt' corresponds to Freud's Oedipal stage.

3.20 Married people are always psychologically healthier and better adjusted than divorced people.

3.21 Freud's first theories about the psychodynamic organisation of the mind have been called the 'affect-trauma model'.

3.22 In performing word fragment completion tasks, the ability to complete the word fragments correctly, immediately after learning the words, shows that explicit memory is intact.

3.23 According to Rank, 'character armour' refers to repetitive unconscious behaviours that protect against both internal and external dangers to the individual.

3.24 Multiple behaviour problems are best treated sequentially rather than simultaneously.

3.25 Humans are born with an innate sense of an all-nurturing caretaker, the 'earth mother archetype' according to Jung.

3.26 Detachment, resistance to encultration and democratic philosophy are some of Maslow's fifteen characteristics of self-actualising people.

3.27 The visual cliff experiment can be used to show that a child of four and a half months has developed a degree of depth perception.

3.28 Julian Rotter's social learning theory rejects the involvement of cognitive factors as a determinant of behaviour.

3.29 Kelly's personal construct theory is an example of the phenomenological approach to the study of personality.

3.30 Bandura's triadic reciprocal determinism is the two-way, tri-directional influences of behaviour, environment and personal variables.

3.31   Observational learning is the same as vicarious learning.

3.32   'Flashbulb memories' for events learned in emotionally charged circumstances are not affected by retrieval failure with time.

3.33   Goffman described the 'betrayal funnel' in his concept of the 'total institution' whereby patients feel they are betrayed by the system by being committed to an institution.

3.34   Costa and McCrea's five universal factors are: neuroticism (N), extraversion (E), openness (O), agreeableness (A) and conscientiousness (C).

3.35   In the 'Little Albert' experiment, the white rat acted as a conditioned stimulus under classical conditioning.

3.36   Eysenck's categorical model of personality has identified three categories of personality: psychotism, neuroticism and extraversion.

3.37   Respondent learning is another term for operant conditioning.

3.38   Carter and McGoldrick divided the family cycle into a six-stage schema based on emotional process.

3.39   Obese individuals tend to view themselves as being thinner than they actually are.

3.40   In solving a problem, when compared to novices, experts tend to reason backward from a solution to the given problem.

3.41   Lidz described 'marital schism' to describe the situation of having a dominating mother and a passive father.

3.42   Social learning theory conceptualises aggression as vicariously learned behaviour, secondary to a frustration-produced drive.

3.43   The Cannon-Bard theory of experience of emotion holds that somatic responses and experience of emotion occur together after an emotive perception.

3.44   When compared to heterosexuals, the exclusively homosexual have been noted to exclusively identify with the same sex parent.

3.45   The 'theory of mind' predicts that a three year old child will successfully predict what another person will think is in a labelled box that has unexpected contents (deceptive box task).

3.46   The Minnesota Multiphasic Personality Inventory (MMPI) has ten clinical scales and three validity scales.

3.47   If an individual is asked to attend to a well-known nursery rhyme being played into the right ear of a headphone, he or she will hear less of an unfamiliar message being played into the left ear, than if an unknown poem were played into the right ear.

3.48	In the Q Sort method of personality testing, all the Q items use nine piles to describe individual items.

3.49	Induction of long-term potentiation, which involves activation of the N-methyl-D-aspartate (NMDA) receptor, is thought to be important in memory formation.

3.50	If one's mother tongue is Chinese and one cannot remember the English word one has learned for an object (instead the Chinese word keeps popping into one's head) then this is an example of retroactive interference.

3.51	Alexithymia was first described by Kraepelin.

3.52	The Kleinian main defences are: omnipotence, denial and idealism.

3.53	'Occupational delirium' was used in the early part of the twentieth century to described delirium caused by exposure to toxic substances that were commonly encountered in some occupations.

3.54	Heinroth's *Verruckheit* was characterised by delusions and auditory hallucinations.

3.55	The term 'carebaria' refers to subjective feelings of discomfort in the buttocks.

3.56	Anhedonia in depression can be viewed as a flattened affect.

3.57	The incorporating of delusions into a more systematised series of beliefs is known as 'delusional work'.

3.58	Bleuler's term 'schism' is a defence mechanism characterised by unconscious splitting.

3.59	Cameron is associated with the term 'schizophasia'.

3.60	Loss of capacity to feel emotions even though a person can express them is an example of depersonalization.

3.61	Perseveration is a pathognomic sign of organic brain disease.

3.62	In schizophrenic depersonalisation, reality testing is impaired.

3.63	When an individual is hypnotised and asked to perform an action after a certain fixed period of time, it is frequently found that the individual's estimation of time is impaired.

3.64	Janet first described the lowering of psychic energy as the main mental mechanism responsible for dissociation.

3.65	Synaesthesiae does not occur in drug-free mentally well individuals.

3.66	All of Kurt Schneider's first rank symptoms arise from loss of ego boundaries.

3.67	Tactile hallucinations are associated with oneiroid states.

3.68 Pareidolia will never occur against a person's will.

3.69 A subjective sense of constriction is characteristic of the mood of anxiety.

3.70 Delusion of enormity is more common in schizophrenia than in affective disorder.

3.71 Porropsia is used as a synonym for micropsia by some authors.

3.72 The use of psychological analgesia for childbirth will result in around a quarter of patients having little or no pain during labour.

3.73 Even non-psychotic individuals may hallucinate if experimenters use suggestion on them.

3.74 Anticipatory anxiety occurs in obsessions, phobia, post-traumatic disorder, and compulsions.

3.75 Night terrors are associated with sleepwalking.

3.76 Phonation is more common in frontal lobe seizures than in temporal lobe seizures.

3.77 Recognition is an important part of the memory process.

3.78 Manic stupor always occurs during the stage of transition between depression and mania.

3.79 The experience of individuals undergoing an ecstatic experience may be described by the German term *Witzelsucht*.

3.80 Manfred Bleuler's fundamental symptoms are based on Freud's psychoanalytical concepts.

3.81 *Flexibilitas cerea* (waxy flexibility) is occasionally associated with frontal lobe tumours.

3.82 Speech confusion is the inability of the patients with receptive aphasia to recognise other peoples's speech.

3.83 Verbigeration (talking past the point) is associated with, but not pathognomic of, Ganser's syndrome.

3.84 The phantom limb phenomenon is an example of sensory deception.

3.85 Apophanous perceptions are sometimes understandable to the clinician if he/she knows the recent mood state of the patient.

3.86 Primary process thinking is non-linear and image oriented.

3.87 Confabulation tends to occur only in the later stages of the Korsakov syndrome.

3.88 Secondary elaboration of a dream does not occur during sleep.

3.89 A reduction in action and speech is a central feature of stupor.

3.90 Jung rejected Freud's idea of libido being responsible for sexual drive, but he believed that libido is the source for other mechanisms apart from sexuality.

3.91 Non-insane automatism refers to automatism that is a result of non-psychiatric causes.

3.92 The persecutory delusions of different disorders can be understood by use of Freud's theory of projection.

3.93 Westphal originally described agoraphobia.

3.94 According to Klein, a child develops its true self as a result of the mother imposing her own needs over those of her child.

3.95 Admission rates to psychiatric hospitals are highest in the late winter/early spring months.

3.96 Resistance to the pathological ideas is not found in delusional mood.

3.97 Unlike pareidolic illusions, affect illusions disappear with closer attention to the observed object.

3.98 Retrospective falsification is an example of confabulation.

3.99 Illusions are examples of sensory distortions.

3.100 Treatment of drug-related parkinsonism with anticholinergics is often unlikely to improve objective symptomatology.

3.101 Risperidone is metabolised by the cytochrome P450 enzyme 2D6 to an active metabolite.

3.102 Maprotiline may be safely used in patients with a history of epilepsy.

3.103 Most typical antipsychotics have inhibitory actions on the pre-synaptic dopamine reuptake transporter as well as their dopamine D_2 receptor antagonism.

3.104 Lorazepam has a higher dependence potential than diazepam.

3.105 After taking similar doses of olanzapine plasma levels tend to be higher in females than in males.

3.106 Renal tubular damage and memory disturbances may occur at therapeutic serum levels of lithium.

3.107 Around 25% of clozapine is excreted unmetabolised in the urine.

3.108 Trimipramine has high histaminergic receptor affinity when compared to amitriptyline.

3.109 Venlafaxine is metabolised by cytochrome P450 2D6 to an inactive metabolite.

3.110 Phenelzine, with a higher affinity to MAO (monoamine oxidase) type A than MAO type B (6:1), has a higher clinical potency than isocarboxazid which has equal affinity to both MAO type A and type B.

3.111 In studies of placebo effect, tablets of either very small size, or of very large size, tend to have greater effect.

3.112 When treating patients with short-term benzodiazepines, the half-life of the drug should be used as a definite index of the duration of action.

3.113 Mirtazepine reduces rapid eye movement (REM) sleep.

3.114 Clomipramine does not have affinity for dopamine D_2 receptors.

3.115 Nefazodone has been reported to cause priapism.

3.116 Clonazepam is associated with inter-dose rebound anxiety.

3.117 In patients maintained on methadone 80–120 mg once daily, peak plasma concentrations are usually in the range of 440–1600 ng/ml.

3.118 Lithium should be continued during the immediate pre-operative period.

3.119 Although an old drug, chloral hydrate remains a suitable hypnotic for a patient with insomnia who has suicidal ideation because of its high safety index.

3.120 Mianserin needs to be used with great caution in patients with a history of impulsive self-harming behaviour.

3.121 Lamotrigine is thought to have effects on voltage-sensitive sodium and calcium channels.

3.122 When compared to standard release lithium preparations, slow release preparations have an increased risk in cases of overdose.

3.123 Remoxipride is available for use as an antipsychotic agent in Great Britain.

3.124 Trifluoperazine, flupenthixol and pipothiazine palmitate all have anti-depressant properties.

3.125 When venlafaxine is given in high doses (above 300 mg daily) there is little inhibition of serotonin reuptake; instead, nor-adrenaline and dopamine reuptake are reduced.

3.126 Combinations of carbamazepine and lithium produce neurotoxic reactions only when either one of the drug levels increases above the normal therapeutic range.

3.127 Thioridazine is associated with retrograde ejaculation.

3.128 β-flupenthixol antagonises serotonin receptors.

3.129 Haloperidol has one important metabolite, reduced haloperidol, which has significant antipsychotic activity.

3.130 Propensity to develop agranulocytosis in treatment with clozapine may be related to genetic predisposition.

3.131 When taken in combination, lithium carbonate tends to counteract the potential of carbamazepine to produce reductions in the white cell count.

3.132 Oxypertine and amisulpride mainly inhibit dopamine.

3.133 Mirtazepine has the effect of inhibiting the reuptake of both noradrenaline and serotonin.

3.134 Haloperidol is more potent than droperidol and benperidol.

3.135 St. John' wort has been found to have beneficial effects on fertility for both males and females.

3.136 Dopamine receptors in human cortex can be visualised by PET studies.

3.137 Nefazodone is thought to be less sedating than trazodone as a consequence of its lower affinity for peripheral α_1-adrenergic receptors.

3.138 Unlike trazodone, chlorpromazine and thioridazine do not cause priapism.

3.139 At a dose of 100 mg twice daily, chlorpromazine exhibits roughly 78% dopamine D_2 receptor occupancy.

3.140 Lithium has no effect on rapid-cycling bipolar affective disorder.

3.141 Risperidone does not produce hyperprolactinaemia.

3.142 When compared to clozapine, tetrabenazine has a potent effect on dopaminergic D_2 receptors.

3.143 Mianserin blocks α_1 and α_2 receptors.

3.144 Risperidone is associated with abdominal pain.

3.145 Zolpidem acts on omega-1, but not omega-2, benzodiazepine receptors.

3.146 When compared to maprotiline, desipramine has less anticholinergic activity.

3.147 Phase II drug trials are trials where the drug is tested on animals with physiological systems thought to be analogous to the system in question in humans.

3.148 During long-term treatment with olanzapine its volume of distribution in the body may increase.

3.149 Lithium clearance tends to be reduced in obese individuals.

3.150 Disulfiram can interfere with thyroid function.

3.151 Asher first coined the term 'Munchausen syndrome by proxy'.

3.152 Specific epileptic personality is more common in uncontrolled epilepsy than in adequately controlled epilepsy.

3.153 Vaughn and Leff have shown that high expressed emotion (EE) increases the risk of relapse in depression.

3.154 Memory disturbances and behavioural changes are the common reasons for the loss of independence in Alzheimer's disease.

3.155 DSM-IV requires that there be a period of at least two weeks in which there are psychotic symptoms in the absence of prominent mood symptoms in order to diagnose schizoaffective disorder.

3.156 When an alcoholic patient reaches the 'readiness for action' stage, according to motivational interviewing, the chance of relapse is low.

3.157 A history of hallucinations and intermittent confusional states in the elderly may suggest a diagnosis of dementia of the Lewy body type.

3.158 Andreason suggested that certain thought disorders are specific to schizophrenia.

3.159 Kraepelin's original description of paraphrenia described the onset generally occurring after the age of 55 and the possibility of the disorder not showing a progressive deterioration.

3.160 Frith thought that the primary defect of schizophrenia, the defective meta-representation, is due to a functional disconnection between the anterior brain and the posterior brain.

3.161 The UK 700 study has shown that there are marked beneficial effects of reduced caseloads in intensive case management of patients with severe psychosis in terms of clinical outcome and cost-effectiveness.

3.162 Molecular genetic studies suggest that bipolar affective disorder is more likely to be a single chromosomal disorder.

3.163 5% of patients who have undergone psychosurgery develop seizures.

3.164 The International Pilot Study of Schizophrenia showed that culture has both pathogenic and pathoplastic effects.

3.165 'Space phobia' describes a fear of falling while walking across a room, for example.

3.166 Rumination is typical of obsessions, anorexia, dysmorphophobia, grief and encephalitis lethargica.

3.167 An individual who accuses himself of having neglected his deceased wife without good cause for this accusation is most likely suffering a pathological (rather than a normal) grief process.

3.168 Deficits in the reward reinforcement mechanism of the social environment may cause unipolar depression.

3.169 Around 15% of bereaved spouses fulfil criteria for a depressive episode two years after their partner died.

3.170 Donald Klein strongly disagrees with the dichotomy concept of depression (neurotic and psychotic types being two separate condition) and believes that the two depressions vary only in severity.

3.171 One in three women who have had puerperal psychosis will have a further episode of puerperal psychosis later in life.

3.172 The risk of developing schizophrenia is less for children reared by their biological parents than for children who are adopted.

3.173 Depersonalisation-derealisation disorder is categorised under dissociative/conversion disorders in ICD-10.

3.174 Albinism and narcolepsy are significantly associated with schizophrenic symptoms.

3.175 In parkinsonism associated with neuroleptic treatment, tremor occurs more frequently than akinesia.

3.176 Levels of carbohydrate-deficient transferrin are useful for screening for heavy alcohol use.

3.177 Guilt as a feature of depression is described as a prominent component of the syndrome in most cultures.

3.178 The psychodynamic theory of Paul Federn describes schizophrenia as a result of loss of energy investments in ego inner boundaries.

3.179 Fatal familial insomnia is thought to be a prion dementia.

3.180 Women have an increased risk to develop alcoholism.

3.181 In paraphrenia, about half of patients will have auditory hallucinations.

3.182 In dissociative amnesia, the memory loss is explicit.

3.183 Suicides increased during the month after the funeral of Diana, Princess of Wales in 1997, particularly among 25–44-year-old women.

3.184 Vivid hallucinations and passivity feelings can occur in dissociative disorder.

3.185 Approximately 20% of patients with bulimia nervosa have been markedly overweight at some stage.

3.186 According to Eysenck, dissocial personality disordered people commonly develop conditioning responses faster than most other people.

3.187 Type A personality has been shown to increase the risk of further adverse cardiac events in individuals with established coronary artery disease.

3.188 According to Parkes, in normal grief reaction, the first stage can occur in the third week after bereavement.

3.189 The risk for suicide remains lower than that for the general population for women during their pregnancy and in the postnatal period.

3.190 Mechanic's concept of illness behaviour does not include illness behaviours without a physical illness.

3.191 When videotaped secretly, mothers who have subjected their child to Munchausen syndrome by proxy are seen to remain over-involved and over-attentive to the child.

3.192 Thought sonarisation occurs in obsessive-compulsive disorder.

3.193 Anticholinergics are not recommended in the treatment of neuroleptic malignant syndrome.

3.194 It was Kleist but not Kahlbaum who thought that the catatonic symptoms are neurological signs.

3.195 About 10% of individuals who have a hypomanic episode will go on to have a manic episode.

3.196 Echo reactions are always characterised by either repeating the same word or actions only.

3.197 Kraepelin's account of manic-depressive insanity is almost identical to current concepts of bipolar affective disorder.

3.198 'Delusional perception' and 'delusional misinterpretation' are synonyms.

3.199 MAOIs taken during pregnancy are associated with placental hypoperfusion.

3.200 Sosias delusions are misidentification of other people, but not the spouse.

Paper Four

4.1 Escape training is another term for avoidance training.

4.2 According to social learning theory, marked differences in their choice of play activities due to presence of an observer are more characteristic in five years old girls than in five years old boys.

4.3 Aptitude refers to an individual's potential ability.

4.4 Unlike Skinner's experiments, Thorndike and Pavlov conducted their experiments mainly on dogs.

4.5 According to Allport's theory of personality, most of us have 5–10 cardinal dispositions that direct many aspects of our lives.

4.6 The rooting reflex of the human infant is an example of 'fixed-action pattern'.

4.7 Eric Berne subdivided the part of the psyche he called the 'child' into three parts: the natural child, the rebellious child and the child-next-door.

4.8 Hippocrates, Theophrastus and Sheldon are 'type theorists' of personality.

4.9 Research suggests that long-term consolidation of memory may require REM (rapid eye movement) sleep.

4.10 The correlation between any two items of Wechsler Adult Intelligence Scale is high.

4.11 Social loafing is seen when focus is placed on the group instead of the individual.

4.12 'Transactional Analysis' is more beneficial in one-to-one evaluation, than in a group setting.

4.13 Marks proposed the 'three pathways model' of phobia development, whereby fears may develop either by direct conditioning, receiving information or vicarious experience.

4.14 The 'Holmes and Rahe Social Readjustment Rating Scale' is same as the 'Holmes and Rahe Life Event Scale'.

4.15 An individual may achieve level III (postconventional morality) on Kohlberg's stages of moral reasoning, despite not having achieved Piaget's formal operational stage of cognitive development.

4.16   A child under the age of six cannot serve as an attachment figure.

4.17   Lesions in the angular gyrus produce an inability to read or write.

4.18   Studies of maternal attachment representations have shown that a positive pattern of representation corresponds to their infant's secure attachment and a reflexive pattern of representation corresponds to their infant's insecure attachment.

4.19   Complex arguments are more likely to be persuasive if the listener is intelligent and has high self-esteem.

4.20   According to Kohlberg, 'moral musical chairs' are the key influencing features of progression from lower to higher stages of moral development.

4.21   Research has shown that working-class neighbourhoods are much more resistant to having psychiatric group homes located nearby than middle-class ones.

4.22   According to Piaget, an eight year old exhibits finalism, syncretism and artificialism.

4.23   Patients from upper social classes are more likely to receive psychological treatments than those from lower social classes.

4.24   Rachman's concept of phobia rejects the possibility of developing fear without a direct contact with the feared object.

4.25   Subliminal signals that take the form of taboo words tend to be more difficult to perceive.

4.26   Freud's structural theory says that 'das Ich' is responsible for secondary processes.

4.27   Vaughan and Leff (1976) showed that praise was associated with high expressed emotion and predicted relapse in patients.

4.28   According to the Sapir-Whorf hypothesis of language, 'linguistic determinism' means that the language spoken by people determines the way they perceive the world.

4.29   Eric Berne introduced the notion of 'the name of the father' into psychoanalytic theory.

4.30   Defensible space in a large housing estate will reduce crime.

4.31   The three types of aversive conditioning are: avoidance conditioning, escape conditioning and punishment.

4.32   In depression, low levels of face-to-face contacts and communications are associated with good outcome.

4.33   There has been little evidence for a major role of life events in the aetiology of puerperal psychosis.

4.34   The post-Freudian Winter found that students with high 'fear of power' were prompt in submitting their major term papers.

4.35 Girls tend to better than boys at arranging blocks in specified patterns.

4.36 Post-Freudians do not consider the 'therapeutic alliance' as a sufficient condition for effective therapy.

4.37 Approximately 5% of children have eidetic imagery.

4.38 Gordon Allport felt that in reality most people do not use a large number of descriptive adjectives.

4.39 Rats who have been subjected to stressful handling experiences when young, show later in life increased fear responses when placed in strange environments.

4.40 According to Reiss's family paradigm model, 'the consensus-sensitive family' is high on co-ordination factor and low on configuration and closure factors.

4.41 In psychology, 'instrumental aggression' is aggressive behaviour that has discomfort of the victim as its principle reward.

4.42 Minuchin's concept of disengagement is the opposite of Stierlin's concept of co-individuation.

4.43 The ancient Greek concept of the 'sanguine' temperament corresponds to the modern classification of temperament category of 'reward dependence'.

4.44 Sheldon's three basic temperament types are: endomorphic, ectomorphic and mesomorphic.

4.45 Self-transcendence is one of the three main character traits described.

4.46 According to Bandura's vicarious learning model, the observer invariably avoids mimicking a model's punished behaviour throughout his life.

4.47 Eric Berne was one of the first psychotherapists to systematically describe guided imagery therapy.

4.48 The Premack principle says that any high frequency behaviours can reinforce lower frequency behaviours only when they are pleasurable.

4.49 Individuals rated to have high reward dependence temperaments have been found to have reduced urine MPHG levels.

4.50 Maslow has described only two kinds of motives as the basic processes operating in his hierarchy of needs.

4.51 Delirium is associated with a true hypoacusis.

4.52 A wealthy women who spends around twelve hours every day working for charities to the exclusion of all other activities, but who views herself as being a devoted wife and mother, is an example of an individual using 'reaction formation' as a defence mechanism.

4.53 An identifiable phrase uttered during an epileptic seizure is an example of a speech automatism.

4.54 The conflict faced by devout Roman Catholics regarding the use of contraception is an example of conflict between ego versus superego mechanisms.

4.55 Generally, the severity of irritability tends to increase proportionally with age.

4.56 'Delusion of unique individuality' is a normal manifestation of interpersonal distress.

4.57 Splitting of perception is quite common in organic conditions such as temporal lobe epilepsy.

4.58 One-trial learning is more complex than other forms of classical conditioning.

4.59 The quality of *publicness* is one quality that has been found to commonly differentiate real from hallucinatory perceptions.

4.60 Dereistic thinking is abnormal thinking.

4.61 'Loss of emotional resonance' is different from the difficulty a therapist can have in empathising with some schizophrenic patients.

4.62 *Verstimmung* is primarily a disturbance of mood.

4.63 The term 'holophrastic' has been used to describe the paucity of meaning that occurs in some speech of patients with schizophrenia.

4.64 In depersonalisation, increased skin conductance measures are the invariable finding.

4.65 Visual hyperaesthesia is especially associated with mania among the functional psychoses.

4.66 Positive transference to an institution is always detrimental to the patient.

4.67 Glossolalia is the utterance of unintelligible words/sounds that are understandable to the speaker but not to the listener.

4.68 Predisposing life events always occur between the birth of an individual and the onset of an illness or a relapse.

4.69 Most hypnopompic hallucinations are probably really hypnagogic hallucinations.

4.70 Individuals who have undergone a near death experience develop a strong sense of purpose and become more materialistically concerned.

4.71 Polyphagia involves the eating of objects that cannot be described as food.

4.72 Bruch did not think of the anorexic behaviour of 'pursuit to thinness' as being a pleasurable experience to the individual.

4.73 In trance, the individual experiences absorption that tends to result in sleepiness.

4.74 Hallucinations are characteristic features of trimethoxyamphetamine, harmine and ibogaine abuse.

4.75 Schneider's *Allgemeine Psychopathologie* (*General Psychopathology*) is an important early work in phenomenology.

4.76 Hypoactivity in the delirious state is very unusual.

4.77 *Wurgstimme* has been used to describe the quality of speech sometimes observed in schizophrenia where the individual speaks with an unusually low voice.

4.78 In Alzheimer's disease, visual hallucinations are less common than auditory hallucinations.

4.79 Auditory hallucinations in the form of short, derogatory comments are relatively common in severe depression.

4.80 Peer group pressure and pleasure play an important role in psychoactive substance abuse.

4.81 Patients who have a high temperature tend to experience time as passing more quickly than it actually is.

4.82 High expressed emotions are unlikely to be a coping style of the relatives living with schizophrenics.

4.83 The term 'catatonic syndrome' is associated with Kiley.

4.84 Reduced speech rate is a very reliable discriminator of melancholic and non-melancholic depression.

4.85 It is rare for exhibitionists to branch out into any other form of sexual perversion.

4.86 Normal shyness and social phobia are qualitatively different.

4.87 Necrophilia is associated with homicide.

4.88 According to DSM-IV, in agoraphobia without history of panic disorder, panic symptoms can occur.

4.89 'Age disorientation' is defined as a three-year discrepancy between actual age, and what the patient states is his/her own age.

4.90 Maher thought that delusions are secondary to real-life

44   *MCQs for the New MRCPsych Part 1*

experiences.

4.91 Patients who have auditory hallucinations tend to be quite distressed by the voices if they cannot determine the gender of the speaker.

4.92 Amnesia occurs in both of the following conditions: middle cerebral artery embolism and anterior cerebral artery haemorrhage.

4.93 Hearing one's name spoken aloud by one's own voice is an example of an auditory form of autoscopic hallucination.

4.94 Depersonalisation disorder is more common in women than in men.

4.95 Narcissism is associated with growing older.

4.96 Activities to reduce an individual's extreme emotional reaction to acute stresses are almost always beneficial to the individual's health.

4.97 In *koro*, the individual may fear that the penis will shrink back up into the brain.

4.98 The most frequent coping strategy in acute reaction to stress is denial.

4.99 Thoughts are held by some to be epiphenomena.

4.100 *Witzelsucht* is a disorder of affect.

4.101 On the electrocardiogram significant shortening of the QT interval by an antipsychotic such as sertindole may lead to *torsade de pointes* which may be fatal.

4.102 Tricyclics interact with clonidine, guanethidine and propranalol.

4.103 Risperidone increases plasma levels of prolactin to the same extent or more than haloperidol.

4.104 Ankle swelling is a common side-effect of valproate.

4.105 Venlafaxine is highly plasma protein bound.

4.106 Phenothiazines may increase the risk of developing cataracts.

4.107 Hong Kong Chinese patients are particularly susceptible to the development of tardive dyskinesia.

4.108 Regarding the metabolism of tricyclic antidepressants, tertiary amines are demethylated to secondary amines, but the reverse reaction never occurs.

4.109 Diphenylbutylpiperidines have structural similarities with the butyrophenones.

4.110 Flupenthixol and pimozide do not have anticholinergic adverse effects.

4.111 Carbamazepine is associated with a decrease in T_3 and T_4.

4.112 Oculodermal melanosis is a recognised syndrome caused by phenothiazines.

4.113 Most studies on the use of β-adrenergic receptor antagonists in controlling aggression have shown that low-dose propranolol is of benefit.

4.114 Chlorpromazine and fluphenazine but not flupenthixol are enzyme inducers.

4.115 In contrast to most benzodiazepines, clorazepate is metabolised in the stomach to its active form and then absorbed into the blood stream.

4.116 T_3 is more effective than T_4 in augmenting the antidepressant effect of tricyclic antidepressants.

4.117 Although experience is limited, since zopiclone is excreted into breast milk in minute quantities, it may be of benefit in the short-term treatment of insomnia in breast-feeding mothers.

4.118 In depression, following ECT, the reduction of noradrenaline levels in plasma and reduction of corticotrophin releasing hormone levels in CSF may offer better prediction of outcome.

4.119 The main difference in the pharmacodynamic profile of nefazo-done and trazodone is that trazodone lacks noradrenaline reuptake inhibitory properties and instead has antihistamine activity.

4.120 Valproate causes hyperammonaemia and glycinaemia.

4.121 To date, quetiapine has been associated with little or no extra-pyramidal side-effects.

4.122 Clozapine is associated with an increased risk of agranulocytosis more in elderly patients than in younger patients.

4.123 Flumazenil is of use in the treatment of benzodiazepine overdose since it is an inverse agonist of the benzodiazepines.

4.124 In a patient with schizophrenia and Parkinson's disease treatment with clozapine never exacerbates parkinsonian symptoms.

4.125 SSRIs are associated with a lower rate of induction of iatrogenic mania than are the tricyclic antidepressants.

4.126 In schizophrenia, the primary pathology is the abnormality of dopamine in the brain.

4.127 The placebo response to painful stimuli may be attenuated by naloxone.

4.128 Chlorpromazine, amitriptyline and loxapine have a tricyclic structure.

4.129 95% of mirtazepine is excreted by the kidneys.
4.130 After antipsychotic withdrawal, prolactin levels return to normal within a very short period.
4.131 Clinical hypothyroidism associated with lithium treatment occurs in 2% of patients.
4.132 Risperidone and quetiapine are best avoided in cardiac patients.
4.133 Sexual dysfunction as a side-effect of selective serotonin reuptake inhibitors is a result of over-stimulation of the $5HT_2$ class of receptors.
4.134 Neuroleptic malignant syndrome is always associated with elevated creatinine phosphokinase levels.
4.135 Rivastigmine is not metabolised by the liver.
4.136 Among secondary amines, protriptyline has the least sedating effect.
4.137 In treatment resistant depression, phenelzine may be combined with clomipramine if the patient is carefully monitored.
4.138 Disulfiram does not interfere with tricyclic antidepressant levels.
4.139 The reputed efficacy of gabapentin in the treatment of bipolar affective disorder is thought to be a result of its acting to inhibit GABA reuptake.
4.140 Oral chlorpromazine is recommended to treat the monoamine oxidise inhibitor induced hypertensive crisis.
4.141 Apart from its hypnotic effects, chloral hydrate has anticonvulsant and analgesic properties.
4.142 Acute dystonias include exaggerated posturing, torticollis and grimacing.
4.143 The elimination half-life of tacrine is roughly 11 hours.
4.144 Gabapentin, a GABA mimetic novel amino acid, is related in structure to GABA.
4.145 Amisulpride blocks mainly D_2 and D_3 receptors.
4.146 Patients who are on treatment with viloxazine or imipramine need a high dose of the oestrogen contraceptive 'pill'.
4.147 When a benzodiazepine binds to the benzodiazepine receptor-binding site it directly affects the chloride channel.
4.148 In akathisia subjective restlessness may be absent and it may be exacerbated by neuroleptic withdrawal.
4.149 Bromocriptine may be beneficial in obsessive-compulsive disorder.
4.150 Hypersomnolence is recognised side-effect of fluoxetine.
4.151 Neuroleptic malignant syndrome usually lasts for 5 to 10 days after

antipsychotics have been discontinued.

4.152 Obsessions and compulsions are not found in mixed anxiety and depressive disorder.

4.153 Immediate intravenous diazepam is the treatment of choice for acute laryngeal dystonia occurring in a young male commenced on haloperidol the day previously.

4.154 Compulsive behaviour is a characteristic feature of Kluver-Bucy syndrome.

4.155 'Hypofrontality' as measured by glucose and oxygen utilisation studies has been reported in patients with bipolar affective disorder.

4.156 *Pavor nocturnus* commonly begins in early adolescence.

4.157 Depressions that are secondary to general medical conditions tend to respond better to treatment than primary depressions.

4.158 The prevalence of schizophrenia in the monozygotic twin of an affected proband and in the children of two schizophrenic parents is the same.

4.159 The MOUSEPAD assessment schedule has sections for determining the degree of symptomatology and functional disturbance in elderly depressed patients.

4.160 Both senile plaques and neurofibrillary tangles contain paired helical filaments.

4.161 Binswanger's disease is associated with gradual onset of dementia and physical features such as gait difficulties.

4.162 Kluver-Bucy syndrome commonly occurs in frontal lobe dementia.

4.163 In paraphrenia, around 15% of patients will have visual hallucinations.

4.164 Common psychiatric sequelae of multiple sclerosis are depression, dementia and euphoria.

4.165 Electroconvulsive therapy is particularly effective in individuals suffering from schizophrenia if they have delusions of passivity.

4.166 Public education on alcohol prevention has been proved to be non-beneficial.

4.167 In patients with schizophrenia, depressive symptoms are more common in females than in males.

4.168 Offenders with a history of alcohol related crime could benefit from controlled drinking practices.

4.169 A course of electroconvulsive therapy leads to an increase in $5HT_2$ receptors.

4.170 Normal pressure hydrocephalus can occur in Alzheimer's disease.

4.171 In adults, the prevalence of simple phobias is roughly similar in males and females.

4.172 Delusions and hallucinations are associated with dialysis.

4.173 Identification phenomena in grief reactions are often considered pathological.

4.174 Violence occurs more commonly in temporal lobe epilepsy.

4.175 CSF 5-HIAA concentrations have been shown to be lower in patients whose weight has returned to normal after the course of anorexia nervosa.

4.176 The most important diagnostic procedure of insomnia is sleep laboratory study.

4.177 According to ICD-10, adjustment disorders must occur within three months of the stressor.

4.178 Depersonalisation is due to a loss of basic mental functions.

4.179 Bloating of the gastrointestinal system with no identifiable medical disorder is more likely to be reported by men then women.

4.180 In premature ejaculation, ejaculation commonly occurs within a minute after penetration.

4.181 Almost 90% of patients complaining of globus have no identifiable medical diagnosis.

4.182 Cocaine use during pregnancy causes urinary tract development defects in the foetus.

4.183 Patients with puerperal mania invariably have disturbed sleep patterns.

4.184 Rebound symptoms which occur after discontinuing benzodiazepines are characterised by the return of original symptoms with the same severity for which the benzodiazepine was used to treat in the first place.

4.185 Patients with factitious disorder who admit readily to their simulation of symptoms have a better prognosis than those who do not admit this.

4.186 On the EEG, some of the non-alcoholic sons of alcoholic fathers show deficiencies of beta waves.

4.187 Trismus is an example of a dystonic reaction to antipsychotic medication affecting the eye muscles.

4.188 Paraphilia is associated with borderline personality disorder.

4.189 As a patient with bipolar affective disorder gets older, the number of manic episodes tends to decrease while the number of depressive episodes increases.

4.190 Primary biliary cirrhosis is associated with generalised anxiety disorder.

4.191 Recurrent brief depressive disorder is included as a category in ICD-10.

4.192 Brain monoamine oxidase levels do not differ between men and women.

4.193 The risk of first-degree relatives developing a depressive illness is roughly the same whether a proband develops depression in early or late life.

4.194 Predisposing factors for rapid-cycling affective disorders include menopause, minor tranquilliser abuse, female gender and hypothyroidism.

4.195 The deep white matter lesions seen on MRI in depressed elderly patients tend to be located in the left basal ganglia.

4.196 Mitochondrial myopathy can present as a dissociative disorder.

4.197 Around 90% of the general population feel that patients with schizophrenia are a danger to others.

4.198 Rapid eye movement sleep changes are specific to melancholic depression.

4.199 The one-year prevalence rate of generalised anxiety disorder in men has been estimated to be 2%.

4.200 In major depression, there is a state-dependent adrenal gland hypertrophy.

Paper Five

5.1 Operant and classical conditioning can be grouped together under the heading 'learning by association'.

5.2 In infants, when compared to the sense of vision, the development of the senses of taste and smell are delayed.

5.3 Democratic leadership styles are the most appropriate if one wants a highly original product.

5.4 According to cognitive-developmental theory, a child is considered to have failed to achieve 'gender identity' if at the age of three years the child can distinguish between pictures of boys and girls but cannot say whether the children in the picture will become mummies or daddies in the future.

5.5 Adolf Meyer pioneered a type of psychodynamic psychotherapy that focussed almost solely on dynamic issues, rather than biological concerns.

5.6 Sensation seeking behaviour is one of Zuckerman's concepts.

5.7 According to Harry Stack Sullivan, 'parataxic' experience involves connected, brief experiences operating outside of the rules of logic.

5.8 Lazarus' cognitive-motivational-relational theory of emotion states that primary appraisal and secondary appraisal act independently of each other.

5.9 Research suggests that operant conditioning only occurs if the animal feels that the reinforcement is under its control.

5.10 According to Hoffman, any types of empathetic responsive behaviours are possible only after the age of two.

5.11 In the classification of territories, secondary territories are places that are accessible to many people but not to all people.

5.12 Category A children with avoidant attachment behaviour are more likely to bully other children.

5.13 Children have been shown to have reduced levels of skin resistance while watching sad scenes in a movie.

5.14 Post-Freudians McClelland and Winter formulated their theories based on power motivation conflicts.

5.15   Thorndike described the process of gradual learning (trial-and-error learning) that takes place in classical conditioning by observing animal experiments.

5.16   Carl Jung's followers always view middle-aged people's 'burn out' experiences as a significant negative development.

5.17   Negative reinforcement plays a role in getting a patient with anorexia nervosa to eat in a ward behavioural regimen designed to get the patient to gain a target weight.

5.18   Gordon Allport's theory states that acts or habits that are inconsistent with a trait are not proof of non-existence of that trait.

5.19   Fechner's law states that sensory perception is an exponential function of stimulus intensity.

5.20   The chance of spousal violence decreases in the wake of a spouse's decision to leave the partner.

5.21   Perceptual constancy is thought to be present at birth in humans.

5.22   Cattell's 16-PF personality test has four sources of data namely: L-data, P-data, N-data and Q-data.

5.23   Mowrer described a two-stage theory for the development of fears.

5.24   Signal detection theory disagrees with the 'absolute threshold model' of sensory stimulus perception in the presence of 'zero stimulus'.

5.25   According to the 'matching hypothesis' individuals try to pair off with the most attractive individual available to them.

5.26   Negative reinforcement invariably increases the likelihood of occurrence of the target behaviour.

5.27   Otto Rank felt that birth trauma was more important in the shaping of personality than the Oedipal complex.

5.28   The 'time-out' techniques that are used to eliminate unwanted behaviour are not useful aversive procedures.

5.29   A basic premise of evolutionary theory is that individuals will evolve to act in the interest of their own species.

5.30   Neo-Piagetians such as Klahr, Case and Mandler do not agree with Piaget on the concept of the 'qualitative discontinuities' of cognitive developments.

5.31   Children of people who have an authoritative style of parenting tend to be competent and responsible but also socially withdrawn and lack spontaneity.

5.32   Sequences of 'mental movements' could be called 'motoric thought'.

5.33 Wynne and Singer are associated with the theory that abnormal communications in the family lead to the development of schizophrenia in the offspring.

5.34 Unlike the previous scale, the recent revision of the Stanford-Binet uses IQ scores.

5.35 Infants develop the ability to differentiate faces around 10 weeks after birth.

5.36 In learning, 'exemplar strategy' works better with typical instances than atypical ones.

5.37 Racial prejudice may be measured on the Borgadus social distance scale.

5.38 Emotional expressions reduce the subjective experience of that emotion.

5.39 The Royal College of Psychiatrists is an example of a 'total institution'.

5.40 The last card in thematic apperception test is a blank card.

5.41 Psychodynamic theory proposes that the chief defence mechanisms that occur in schizophrenia are reaction formation and splitting.

5.42 According to the 'safety signal hypothesis', a housewife is not meant to have a safety signal when her bullying husband is out of town.

5.43 The term 'bottom-up processing' refers to the type of minimal processing that occurs when one develops a mental representation of a sensory experience.

5.44 Kubler-Ross's 'phases of dying' and Murray Parkes's 'phases of grief' disagree in some regards with John Bowlby's separation anxiety concept.

5.45 In language development, when a child uses the word 'doggie' to mean a cat or a cow as well as a dog, this is an example of an *overextension*.

5.46 Ainsworth coined the term 'the rejection syndrome' to indicate the aversion behaviour of mothers of infants with avoidant attachment.

5.47 Freud felt that the newborn infant had a very primitive ego structure in place.

5.48 In England and Wales, the Office of the Population Census and Surveys has classified the unemployed as social class V.

5.49 A clinician does a school visit to observe a child suspected of having a hyperkinetic disorder. The teacher notes that the child was much quieter than usual, tending to observe the doctor during the class. This is an example of the Hawthorne effect.

5.50 In trace conditioning the unconditioned stimulus precedes and ends before the onset of conditioned stimulus.

5.51 Early phenomenologists used the term *'Prüfung'* to describe an excessive anxiety reaction in an individual to a specific stimulus.

5.52 Psychological pillow is not a form of stereotypy.

5.53 Depressed states are particularly associated with noesis.

5.54 Hug-Hellmuth, Klein, Anna Freud and Winnicott developed play techniques.

5.55 According to Schneider, desultory thinking in schizophrenia is characterised by speech that appears normal apart from the sudden occurrence of unrelated ideas in the narrative from time to time.

5.56 An artist, in contrast to a psychiatrist, cannot distinguish the communicatory smile of depression from that of genuine cheerfulness.

5.57 *Pseudologia fantastica* is a common but not pathognomic sign in Korsakov syndrome.

5.58 Thought alienation is not found in obsessions.

5.59 Janet considered *incompleteness* the main experience of those suffering from obsessional neurosis.

5.60 The last three stages of Erikson's eight stages of psychosocial development roughly correspond to the stages of Adolf Meyer.

5.61 Anankastic personality traits include insecurity and insensitivity.

5.62 Retrospective delusions are not paramnesias.

5.63 The hallucinations associated with narcolepsy are more often of the hypnagogic than the hypnopompic type.

5.64 Elation as a symptom found in various disorders, is commonly associated with cheerfulness and flight of ideas.

5.65 Reality testing is diminished in hypnosis.

5.66 Verbal stereotypy is a form of perseveration.

5.67 Continuous derogatory hallucinatory comments are characteristic of a severe depressive episode with psychotic features.

5.68 Conrad's 'apophenia' is a primary delusion.

5.69 One can empathise with a patient's psychotic experience even when one has never had a psychotic episode.

5.70 Corrective emotional experience is the outcome of transference neurosis.

5.71 Lilliputian hallucinations are usually associated with marked anxiety in individuals experiencing them.

5.72 The concrete thinking that occurs in schizophrenia is no different from the concrete thinking that can occur in neurotic conditions.

5.73 Seeing one's double (Doppelganger) is an example of an autoscopic hallucination.

5.74 Mitmachen is a mild form of catalepsy.

5.75 All illusions are distinguished by the fact that they disappear when one concentrates on them.

5.76 Transition from pseudohallucination to true hallucination, if this occurs, will never be gradual.

5.77 Behaviour tends to be markedly disorganised in individuals who are undergoing a 'twilight state'.

5.78 Katathymic amnesia is more common in dissociative disorders.

5.79 True delusions cannot be deduced from another morbid phenomenon.

5.80 Schneider called depression with nihilistic ideas 'vital hypochondriacal depression'.

5.81 Cryptamnesia is a term used to describe subclinical amnesia in early Alzheimer's disease.

5.82 The wrinkling of the nose in disgust at a hallucinatory unpleasant smell some patients with severe depression have has been called *Schnauzkrampf*.

5.83 In a familiar situation, when one feels that one has never experienced that particular situation before, the experience is known as *jamais vu*.

5.84 *Sperrung* is not thought blocking but rather motor blocking.

5.85 Twilight states tend to start and end gradually.

5.86 The reduplication phenomenon is a perceptual disorder.

5.87 Attention is increased in absorption.

5.88 Depersonalisation found in schizophrenia is not uncommonly due to depressed mood.

5.89 The excess of winter births seen in schizophrenia is more pronounced in individuals without a family history of schizophrenia.

5.90 Echolalia occurs in learning disability, schizophrenia, Huntington's chorea, factious disorders and mania.

5.91 It is thought that sleepwalking is an acting-out of a concurrent dream.

5.92 *Belle indifference* can be a feature of hysteria, somatisation disorder, latah and frontal lobe tumours.

5.93 Electroencephalographic studies have found no differences in cerebral electrical activity between states of relaxed wakefulness and a state of hypnosis.

5.94 General systems theory stresses the importance of understanding the individual by considering the individual's influence on the whole system.

5.95 Intense emotions are considered to be important in the formation of illusions.

5.96 Occasionally, an overvalued idea can be rational.

5.97 Independence of the will is one of the qualities Jaspers considered to differentiate pseudohallucinations from mental images.

5.98 Bleuler's fundamental symptoms were deemed to have a central psychopathological role.

5.99 Binswanger made important contributions to psychopathological theory.

5.100 Apraxia may result from incoordination.

5.101 When cigarette smoking reduces olanzapine levels in a patient, it does this by induction of the cytochrome P450 2D6 isoenzyme.

5.102 In the central nervous system, MAO-B acts on dopamine, tyramine and noradrenaline.

5.103 The elimination half-life of venlafaxine is about 3½ hours.

5.104 Benztropine may restore erectile function in patients who are on treatment with antipsychotics.

5.105 Pimozide tends to be more sedating than haloperidol.

5.106 Pimozide, thioridazine, trifluoperazine and fluphenazine are calcium channel blockers.

5.107 The percentage of platelet MAO inhibited by an MAOI antidepressant is a good indication of the level of central inhibition of MAO-A.

5.108 β-adrenergic agonists are the drugs of choice to treat antipsychotic-induced hypotension.

5.109 Patients with parkinsonism as a result of treatment with dopamine receptor antagonists usually have a positive glabella tap.

5.110 Molindone, a dihydroindole derivative, is structurally related to the hallucinogen dimethyltryptamine.

5.111 Physostigmine is a safe and convenient treatment for anticholinergic intoxication.

5.112 Amperozide and savoxepine are dopamine antagonists.

5.113 The barbiturates are associated with increased folate metabolism.

5.114 When compared to other antipsychotics, the benzamides (ex. sulpiride) are more hydrophilic and when compared to traditional antipsychotics they show less inter-individual variation in plasma levels.

5.115 Parenteral administration of an anticholinergic for an acute dystonic reaction typically has full effect in 10 to 15 minutes.

5.116 Carbamazepine enhances the re-uptake of dopamine and blocks its release.

5.117 Norfluoxetine has similar potency for serotonin reuptake inhibition as fluoxetine has.

5.118 When leucopenia develops, carbamazepine should be automatically discontinued.

5.119 A tricyclic antidepressant may be given in a depot form.

5.120 Tardive dyskinesia has been reported with reserpine and oxypertine.

5.121 Haloperidol has little α_1-adrenergic antagonism.

5.122 Lithium should not be introduced to a patient receiving more than 20 mg per day of haloperidol.

5.123 Citalopram is the most selective drug of the selective serotonin reuptake inhibitor class.

5.124 Chronic treatment with combined neuroleptic and anticholinergic drugs is associated with an increased prevalence of tardive dyskinesia.

5.125 The finding of low plasma levels of homovanillic acid in some patients with schizophrenia who have predominantly positive symptoms provides support for the dopamine hypothesis of schizophrenia.

5.126 Droperidol, a butyrophenone, has a pronounced hypotensive effect.

5.127 There is reasonable evidence that moclobemide has greater efficacy than SSRIs in the treament of atypical depression.

5.128 Lithium toxicity can occur at normal lithium levels.

5.129 One of the advantages monoamine oxidase inhibitors have over selective serotonin inhibitors is that they have few adverse effects on sexual function.

5.130 Trazodone is contraindicated in patients with a history of glaucoma or prostatic hypertrophy.

5.131 Loxapine is considered an 'atypical' antipsychotic by some experts as it has both serotonin and dopamine antagonism activity.

5.132 Prochlorperazine is a commonly used anti-emetic as its use is not associated with increased risk of teratogenicity.

5.133 Donepezil, unlike tacrine, inhibits acetylcholinesterase preferentially over pseudocholinesterase.

5.134 Among all anticonvulsants, carbamazepine may be the safest anticonvulsant to take during pregnancy.

5.135 Naltrexone antagonises all types of opioid receptor, but has the highest antagonistic properties at the δ-receptor.

5.136 Tics, grunting vocalisations and hemiballismus can be manifestations of tardive dyskinesia.

5.137 Lithium is associated with a lowering of the seizure threshold.

5.138 Anticonvulsants can cause an exacerbation of seizures or status epilepticus.

5.139 The incidence of seizures in patients taking clozapine at more than 600 mg per day is roughly 15%.

5.140 Leucopenia is not an uncommon adverse effect of carbamazepine.

5.141 Paraldehyde is almost completely excreted by the kidneys.

5.142 The REM sleep suppression effect of zopiclone is comparable to the REM sleep suppression effect of benzodiazepines.

5.143 Serotonin-dopamine antagonists allow more dopaminergic transmission in the nigrostriatal pathway than conventional antipsychotic because the normal inhibitory action of serotonin on dopamine neurons is inhibited.

5.144 Serum levels of tricyclic antidepressants above 350 ng/ml are cardiotoxic.

5.145 Piracetam is an example of a nootropic drug, which are drugs that have been found to enhance learning in animal studies.

5.146 Valproic acid may elevate urinary ketones on laboratory tests.

5.147 As a side-effect of dopamine receptor antagonists, akathisia appears most commonly after the third day of initiation of treatment.

5.148 Cyproheptadine, an antihistamine, worsens the adverse effects on male sexual function caused by selective serotonin reuptake inhibitors.

5.149 Bupropion is an antidepressant that is reputed to have a lower risk of 'switching' patients with bipolar affective disorder from a depressive episode into a manic episode.

5.150 Premature ejaculation is a recognised adverse effect of fluoxetine.

5.151 Kendler has shown the hereditability of generalised anxiety disorder to be in the region of 60%.

5.152 Immunosuppression in depression is found to be mainly associated with depressions that are characterised by marked feelings of hopelessness and helplessness.

5.153 ICD-10 includes a category for and a definition of premenstrual tension.

5.154 Opiate abuse affects the immune system by increasing immunoglobulin levels.

5.155 Hypertension is associated with the personality trait of submissiveness.

5.156 In a co-dependency relationship, people living together equally take care of each other at the expense of other social relationships.

5.157 From primate studies, the physiological changes that characterise the acute separation response are almost the opposite of those of the bereavement period.

5.158 In malingering, symptom removal is common by hypnosis, but not by suggestion.

5.159 Puerperal mania is almost invariably followed by a depressive episode before returning to euthymia.

5.160 Transference in a therapeutic relationship is often repetitive and inappropriate.

5.161 Dissociative fugue is commoner in males.

5.162 In intractable mood disorders, imaging studies have failed to show any dysfunction of the brain.

5.163 It is rare for mania to occur in patients for the first time in the seventh or eighth decade.

5.164 In DSM- IV, one may code panic attacks as a separate disorder.

5.165 In the elderly, the proportion of patients with psychotic depression who show non-suppression on the dexamethasone suppression test tends to be higher than the proportion of non-suppressors in those with non-psychotic depression.

5.166 Cerebrospinal fluid serotonin metabolites are increased in manic states.

5.167 Signs of *Psilocybe semilanceata* use include enlarged pupils that are unreactive to light.

5.168 Cryptic bipolar disorders are phenotypically unipolar depression but could be genotypically bipolar.

5.169 Electroconvulsive therapy is associated with a mortality rate of approximately 1 in 10,000 treatments.

5.170 Chronic mania can be secondary to comorbid cerebral pathology.

5.171 Patients with schizophrenia are prone to nightmares.

5.172 High levels of tolerance occur to opioid actions such as meiosis, analgesia and sedation.

5.173 Most individuals with kleptomania describe the impulse to steal as pleasurable.

5.174 Caffeine withdrawal can occur in those who regularly drink 100 mg of caffeine every day.

5.175 Attempted suicide of the mother followed infanticide in about a quarter of cases in one study.

5.176 Co-morbid psychiatric disorders in cocaine abuse are often preceded by cocaine use.

5.177 Munchausen syndrome is commoner in males.

5.178 Chronic use of cannabis is associated with cerebral impairment.

5.179 A period of mild depression precedes approximately half of manic illnesses.

5.180 In Addison's disease, psychotic symptoms are infrequent.

5.181 Once the diagnosis of Alzheimer's disease has been made, female sufferers tend to live longer than male sufferers.

5.182 Posttraumatic headaches do not occur after fourteen days after head injury.

5.183 Some studies have suggested that breast-feeding is protective against developing schizophrenia.

5.184 The DSM-IV subtypes of anorexia nervosa are: the restricting type and the bulimic/purging type.

5.185 A modest, but statistically significant, benefit was seen in the treatment group in the only double-blind study of stereotactic subcaudate tractotomy for obsessive-compulsive disorder.

5.186 Sleep bruxism disorder can cause severe dental damage.

5.187 Detailed interviews tend to show that most patients tend to associate the onset of agoraphobia with an initial panic attack.

5.188 Persons with schizoid personality disorder have increased sensitivity to rejection.

5.189 Up to 26% of patients with anorexia nervosa have comorbid obsessive-compulsive disorder.

5.190 Human immunodeficiency virus (HIV) infection is a common cause of dementia.

5.191 In its classification of standard personality disorders, DSM-IV includes the category of 'passive-aggressive personality disorder', which is not included in ICD-10.

5.192 In Wernicke's encephalopathy, ophthalmoplegia and nystagmus resolve completely after treatment with thiamine.

5.193 Diurnal mood variation is described especially in melancholic depression.

5.194 Apathy and aggression are features of frontal lobe lesions.

5.195 Severe depression is the commonest psychiatric condition associated with the Diogenes syndrome.

5.196 The proportion of people in Northern Ireland who remain sober is higher than the proportion of people remaining sober in (the rest of) Great Britain.

5.197 The auditory hallucinations that occur in dissociative identity disorder (multiple personality disorder) are usually experienced by patients as coming from within themselves.

5.198 Just one session of counselling can significantly influence levels of alcohol consumption in an individual.

5.199 'Medication-induced movement disorders' is included in DSM-IV as a diagnostic category.

5.200 Drug overdose in heroin users is commonly related to intentional behaviour.

Answers to
Question Papers

Answers One

1.1   **True.** This is the process where the group hopes that individuals will get together and come up with a new solution for the whole group. **[J. p122]**

1.2   **False.** A carefully designed study showed that infants who were only 36 hours old could imitate adult facial expressions. **[EE. p78]**

1.3   **True.** The other stages are: anti-locution, avoidance, discrimination and physical attack. **[G. p223]**

1.4   **True.** This age specific response is characteristic, this even occurs in blind infants. **[EE. p97]**

1.5   **True.** Also known as all-or-none reasoning. **[O. p295]**

1.6   **False.** He felt that this is impossible. **[LL. p12–13]**

1.7   **False.** The adult pattern of attachment behaviour that corresponds to the childhood disorganised-disorientated type is the unresolved-disorganised type. **[P. p206]**

1.8   **True. [LL. p72]**

1.9   **False.** Frankl developed this; Janov is associated with the development of primal therapy. **[M. p78]**

1.10   **False.** This need not be by a medical professional. **[FF. p319]**

1.11   **True.** Acquired division of the corpus callosum makes it difficult to feel an object with the left hand and describe it verbally. **[W. p499]**

1.12   **True. [G. p328]**

1.13   **False.** Only traits that the individual is conscious of can be explored. **[G. p281]**

1.14   **True. [EE. p258]**

1.15   **False.** The cognitive triad is of negative views of self, current experience and future. **[O. p11]**

1.16   **False.** These illusion experiments show how size constancy can be broken down. **[EE. p190]**

1.17   **False.** This is more characteristic of the 'paranoid-schizoid position'. **[K. p39]**

1.18   **True. [LL. p24–25]**

1.19   **False.** It becomes invested in the ego; Freud thought that narcissism might account for many conditions such as schizophrenia. **[I. p579]**

1.20 **True.** They merge with one another. **[G. p268–9]**

1.21 **False.** Groupthink is the term given to the tendency of groups to reach a consensus in decisions with individuals putting aside any differing ideas they may have as a result of the forcefulness of the leader or because time is limited for example. **[M. p24]**

1.22 **True. [LL. p200]**

1.23 **False.** This has been shown for those who have hallucinations in schizophrenia as opposed to patients with this diagnosis but without hallucinations: it supports the idea that hallucinations are associated with subvocalisation. **[DD. p175]**

1.24 **True. [U. p10]**

1.25 **False.** Strongly internalised pro-social reasoning is the highest stage and is usually attained around the age of sixteen upwards (if at all). **[G. p242]**

1.26 **False.** It is the gap between the understanding of social processes and the stage actually reached in culture. **[A. p12]**

1.27 **True.** This refers to a mother who puts her own wishes above those of her infant. It contrasts to the notion of the 'good-enough mother'. **[M. p77]**

1.28 **False.** These depend on the nature of illness. **[U. p72]**

1.29 **True.** It appears professional musicians tend to process music mainly with their left hemispheres. **[W. p496]**

1.30 **True. [A. p35]**

1.31 **True. [FF. p116]**

1.32 **False.** They do not focus on divergent thinking. **[G. p406]**

1.33 **True.** Thus individuals improve their performance in remembering items when given cues to help them recall the items. **[I. p33]**

1.34 **True. [JJ. p68]**

1.35 **False.** This is not the case now (2000) as it is currently norm-referenced, but the situation will change shortly. Although this is not a curriculum-based question, it is obviously a fact you should know. **[U. p23]**

1.36 **False.** This is the only truly successful defence mechanism. **[JJ. p93–4]**

1.37 **True. [EE. p142]**

1.38 **True. [FF. p139]**

1.39 **False.** There are higher response rates at the times when the reinforcement is expected. **[M. p3]**

1.40 **False.** Robert White developed this theory. **[JJ. p124–6]**

1.41 **True. [I. p444]**

1.42 **False.** This is the most important form of unconscious resistance. **[JJ. p159]**

1.43 **False.** *Cardinal* numbers. A child will now not make the mistake that there are more counters when spread out in a straight line, having been grouped in two corresponding rows beforehand. **[I. p405]**

1.44 **True. [MM. p9–10]**

1.45 **False.** It is a self-report questionnaire. **[U. p75]**

1.46 **False.** By Erich Lindemann. **[MM. p71]**

1.47 **False.** They give rise to submission. **[M. p13]**

1.48 **True. [JJ. p254]**

1.49 **True. [K. p32]**

1.50 **False.** The opposite is true. **[JJ. p254]**

1.51 **True.** As are organic conditions and schizophrenia. **[Q. p80]**

1.52 **False.** If there is a plastic resistance then it is waxy flexibility. **[Q. p101]**

1.53 **True.** Flattening refers to a diminishment in the range of emotional reaction, whereas blunting refers to marked diminishment of emotional sensitivity. **[H. p278]**

1.54 **True.** E. Bleuler used this term. **[Q. p74]**

1.55 **True.** Despite not being actually pregnant. **[I. p686]**

1.56 **False.** It is a form of verbal stereotypy. **[X. p8]**

1.57 **True.** It is the inability to walk or stand normally. **[I. p679]**

1.58 **True.** This means hallucinatory voices. **[X. p5]**

1.59 **False.** Cameron used this term. **[Q. p49]**

1.60 **False.** This involves auditory recognition. **[U. p91]**

1.61 **False.** It is not unusual to be able to get a reasonable idea of what the neologism means to the patient by being able to identify the elements from other words that may have been fused together. **[Q. p53]**

1.62 **False.** But restlessness in other body parts is. **[NN. p1618]**

1.63 **True.** This is the feeling that large periods of one's life are being recalled rapidly. **[H. p56]**

1.64 **False. [NN. p1819]**

1.65 **True.** Age disorientation is a five-year difference between the correct age of the patient and the age the patient believes he is. **[H. p66]**

1.66 **True.** Kurt Eissler thought so. **[NN. p1616]**

1.67 **True.** It occurs when an individual is unable to recognise a part of his body as being part of him. **[I. p687]**

1.68 **False.** Conrad used this to indicate patients who found vorbeireden amusing. **[Q. p53]**

1.69 **True.** However to varying degrees. This is an example of an 'always' MCQ that is not automatically false. **[Q. p77]**

1.70 **False.** The division is mainly based on the content of emotion. **[Q. p65]**

1.71 **False.** The patient turns towards the interviewer: it is another motor disorder particularly seen in catatonia. **[H. p337]**

1.72 **True. [X. p22]**

1.73 **False.** It usually is appropriate and has purpose although the individual is unaware of it. **[H. p33]**

1.74 **True. [J. p28]**

1.75 **False.** They tend to occur only when the normal perception is in the background. **[H. p39]**

1.76 **False. [I. p1547]**

1.77 **False.** Under-inclusiveness instead. **[H. p310]**

1.78 **True.** This is a form of malingering. **[I. p1616]**

1.79 **True. [H. p303]**

1.80 **True. [I. p1726]**

1.81 **False.** They can occur without any effort on the individual's part, but tend to become clearer the more one focuses on them. **[Q. p17]**

1.82 **False.** Only the neuroses. **[J. p173–4]**

1.83 **True.** Usually brief auditory and visual hallucinations. **[Q. p21]**

1.84 **False.** They are 'ego-dystonic'. **[X. p14–5]**

1.85 **True.** Also known as pathological intoxication. **[H. p35]**

1.86 **False. [J. p25]**

1.87 **False.** The level at which noise becomes unpleasant for the individual instead is lowered. **[H. p79]**

1.88 **True.** This is a synonym for disorder of abstract thinking. **[Q. p48]**

1.89 **False.** To the individual, hallucinations are by definition indistinguishable from real perceptions. **[H. p83]**

1.90 **True.** Astrup reported this. **[Q. p50–1]**

1.91 **False.** The distinction is attenuated. **[H. p45]**

1.92 **False.** They are misused words with no psychiatric significance. **[Q. p53–4]**

1.93 **True.** As has confabulation. **[Q. p7]**

1.94 **False.** This has been reported after removal of eyes. **[X. p20]**

1.95 **False.** This is ambitendence. **[X. p19]**

1.96 **True. [I. p1619]**

1.97 **False.** The former term describes the experience of hearing one's thoughts spoken aloud *while* one is thinking them, while the latter refers to hearing them *after* the thought has passed. [**Q. p23**]

1.98 **False.** Loosening of association and autism are also found in Type I schizophrenia as well. [**F. p77**]

1.99 **True.** [**U. p85**]

1.100 **True.** [**J. p50**]

1.101 **False.** Clozapine levels may be increased by fluvoxamine but the main mechanism is via 3A4 inhibition. [**S. p105**]

1.102 **True.** [**B. p111**]

1.103 **True.** This can lead to peripheral neuropathy. [**I. p2405**]

1.104 **True.** [**E. p189**]

1.105 **False.** Metabolism of methadone tends to increase in the third trimester, so higher doses may be necessary. [**I. p2423**]

1.106 **True.** [**II. p174**]

1.107 **False.** They are all well absorbed: slowing of gastrointestinal transit time will enhance absorption. [**E. p35**]

1.108 **False.** They are slightly less potent than phentolamine. [**B. p102**]

1.109 **True.** [**I. p2282**]

1.110 **False.** This paradoxical finding is explained by the trough in serum levels each day. [**II. p207**]

1.111 **False.** It has no effect on carbamazepine levels, although it can lower valproate levels somewhat. [**I. p2302**]

1.112 **True.** [**OO. p218–9**]

1.113 **False.** Its $5HT_3$ receptor antagonism is responsible for this. [**Y. p74**]

1.114 **False.** It reduces first pass metabolism. [**U. p161**]

1.115 **True.** Brewed tea contains 25–55 mg per 100 ml while brewed coffee has 55–85 mg. [**OO. p109**]

1.116 **False.** Stopping clozapine may prevent progression to agranulocytosis but this doesn't eliminate the risk. [**X. p584**]

1.117 **False.** It does inhibit it, but only to a minor degree. [**Y. p60**]

1.118 **True.** [**X. p539**]

1.119 **False.** Nortriptyline. [**E. p190**]

1.120 **False.** Its use is contraindicated in Addison's disease, myasthenia gravis, glaucoma and bone marrow depression. [**X. p555**]

1.121 **True.** It thus may have antidepressant activity. [**S. p90**]

1.122 **False.** Anecdotal reports indicate it has more efficacy in controlling tremors than other motoric adverse effects. [**NN. p1920**]

1.123 **True.** [**T. p266**]

1.124 **False.** Even though they have higher affinity for D_2 receptors, a

higher risk of movement disorder has not been specifically attribu-
ted. **[B. p104]**

1.125   **False.** The rapid blockade of D_2 receptors leads initially to an increase in dopamine activity. **[Z. p108]**

1.126   **True.** Digoxin inhibits Na^+/K^+-ATPase whereas lithium increases Na^+/K^+-ATPase, which may correlate positively with its clinical effect. **[II. p196]**

1.127   **False.** They antagonise $5HT_{2A}$ heteroreceptors. **[S. p58]**

1.128   **True.** **[II. p317]**

1.129   **True.** **[I. p2369]**

1.130   **False.** **[II. p351]**

1.131   **False.** Decreased motor activity. **[I. p2366]**

1.132   **True.** **[NN. p1990]**

1.133   **False.** It has been reputed to speed up the action of SSRIs by blocking presynaptic $5HT_{1A}$ autoreceptors. **[T. p278]**

1.134   **False.** **[NN. p1996]**

1.135   **True.** The endocannabinoids bind to the naturally occurring cannabinoid receptors of which there are so far two subtypes: CB1 and CB2. **[T. p516]**

1.136   **True.** They are forms of negative attitude to drug treatment, which represent the nocebo component of treatment. **[II. p88]**

1.137   **True.** As is venlafaxine. **[I. p2427]**

1.138   **True.** As oxazepam is more slowly absorbed than diazepam. **[II. p42]**

1.139   **True.** It is especially associated with doses above 300 mg per day: around 13% of patients receiving more than this dose will develop it. **[I. p2430]**

1.140   **False.** They are uncommon. The commonest GI adverse effect is nausea. **[NN. p2116]**

1.141   **False.** Dryness of the mouth is one of the most common side-effects patients on placebo complain of. Other side-effects encountered are: drowsiness, nausea and headache. **[Z. p91]**

1.142   **False.** Smaller tablets are viewed as more potent. **[V. p311]**

1.143   **True.** Some frontal lobe functions will be impaired by D_2 blockers; mesolimbic dopamine blockade is thought to be the most important for control of positive psychotic symptoms. **[S. p41]**

1.144   **False.** Postural hypotension and some reduction in pulse rate are reported. **[X. p567]**

1.145   **True.** It has moderate affinity for D_2 receptors apart from its partial agonism at $5\text{-}HT_{1A}$ receptors. **[I. p2330]**

1.146   **False.** It is demethylation of the side-chain that converts tertiary compounds to secondary amines. Hydroxylation is the rate-limiting step but largely converts tertiary amines to unconjugated forms. **[B. p101]**

1.147 False. Only negligible amounts are. **[I. p2362]**

1.148 False. The risk is inversely associated with age. **[B. p94]**

1.149 True. [E. p120]

1.150 False. Fluoxamine may reduce the clearance of diazepam and thus its half-life is increased. **[II. p178]**

1.151 False. Meduna induced seizures by chemical means. **[C. p220]**

1.152 False. One sexual symptom among a total of eight symptoms is necessary. **[F. p127]**

1.153 True. [C. p276]

1.154 False. Intoxication due to prescribed drugs! **[B. p288]**

1.155 False. DSM-IV classifies the obsessive-compulsive disorders as a subdivision of the anxiety disorders. **[X. p162]**

1.156 True. This is the only specific phobia that has later onset. **[NN. p1207]**

1.157 True. [X. p173]

1.158 False. They more likely to become homosexual. **[NN. p1340]**

1.159 True. However not all researchers have found this association. **[I. p1954]**

1.160 False. Increased dopamine activity in delirium tremens. **[B. p342]**

1.161 False. Increased total REM sleep has been described in bereaved and depressed widows. **[I. p1978]**

1.162 True. [B. p333]

1.163 True. [I. p1665]

1.164 False. It can occur up to 14 days in withdrawal states. **[B. p344]**

1.165 False. It is commoner in females and tends to be characterised by 'atypical' depressive symptoms. **[A. p440]**

1.166 True. [F. p117]

1.167 True. The range given is 10–20%. **[A. p430]**

1.168 True. It is due to a deficit in temporal awareness. **[B. p284]**

1.169 True. A number of studies have shown a correlation between late-onset depression and higher recurrence risk. **[L. p47]**

1.170 False. It includes both temporal lobe and frontal lobe seizures. **[B. p315]**

1.171 False. Around 10–15% do. **[N. p52]**

1.172 True. The onset in men is over the age of 40 and in women is under the age of 30. **[B. p438]**

1.173 True. He is associated with psychodynamic theories of the pathogenesis of diseases such as ulcerative colitis. **[I. p1766]**

1.174 False. ICD-10 lists 'ego-dystonic sexual orientation' as a category, which could also include heterosexuals who are distressed with their heterosexuality. **[NN. p1322]**

1.175 True. Also granular lymphocyte numbers and activity. **[I. p1771]**

1.176 False. They have more grey matter and less white matter. **[NN. p1219]**

1.177 False. M. E. JanWise, F. Mackie, A. C. Zamar, J. P. Watson. Investigation of the 'cuff' method for assessing seizure duration in electroconvulsive therapy. Psychiatric Bulletin 2000; 24: 301. The authors found no significant difference in seizure duration between cuffed and uncuffed limbs.

1.178 False. They are often preferential rather than exclusive. **[NN. p1341]**

1.179 True. Compared with less than 1% of controls. **[C. p909]**

1.180 False. Detached behavior is characteristic of schizoid personality disorder. **[X. p112]**

1.181 False. They tend to have more positive as opposed to negative symptoms. **[A. p460]**

1.182 True. [NN. p1075]

1.183 False. Four days. Don't trust the advice that you only have to know one classification system: you should have detailed knowledge of at least one, but some familiarity with the other. **[HH. p338]**

1.184 True. [NN. p1084]

1.185 False. The plasma levels of GABA tend to be raised. **[I. p1727]**

1.186 True. [NN. p1070]

1.187 False. More in the region of a half of all patients. **[I. p1723]**

1.188 False. These are more common in generalised anxiety disorder. **[NN. p1241]**

1.189 True. It is probably less severe in terms of symptoms in the elderly also. **[N. p140]**

1.190 True. Around 75% has been suggested. **[B. p291]**

1.191 True. [N. p234]

1.192 False. In frontal seizures prolactin level is unreliable. **[B. p318]**

1.193 True. Jones JM, Lawson ML, Daneman D, Olmstead MP, Rodin G. Eating disorders in adolescent female with and without type 1 diabetes: cross-sectional study. BMJ 2000; 320: 1563–1566.

1.194 False. But lower educational and lower income levels predicted this. **[NN. p764]**

1.195 True. Avery and Winokur 1976. **[C. p226]**

1.196 True. [NN. p932]

1.197 False. Factitious disorders lie beyond the sick role although they are abnormal illness behaviours. **[I. p1533]**

1.198 True. [NN. p1020]

1.199 True. However there have been few large studies on this. **[I. p1568]**

1.200 False. The approximate prevalences are: avoidant 1.3%, anankastic 2–6%. **[X. p119]**

Answers Two

2.1   **True.** [I. p572]

2.2   **False.** A child achieves 'conservation of weight' at the age of nine. [EE. p85]

2.3   **False.** Symbolic representation, where innocent objects are used to represent ideas or objects that are in the unconscious. [I. p571]

2.4   **True.** According to Fechner's law, increasing the physical intensity of a stimulus has this effect after an initial rapid increase in perception. [EE. p130]

2.5   **False.** The reverse is true: we tend to give too much weight to the person in making an attribution (dispositional attribution). [EE. p722]

2.6   **True.** [JJ. p154–5]

2.7   **True.** [I. p626]

2.8   **True.** [JJ. p129]

2.9   **False.** 'Superiority' and a 'sense of mastery' are gained through social interest and activity, according to Adler. 'Inferiority' leads to a lack of social interest and thus, a vicious circle. [I. p619]

2.10   **False.** Sudden infant death syndrome is associated with a higher incidence of intense grief. [MM. p79–80]

2.11   **True.** [U. p2]

2.12   **False.** There are two types of behaviour pattern: 'achievement strivings' and 'impatience irritability' types. [JJ. p199–200]

2.13   **False.** This a Likert scale, a Thurstone scale indicates only agreement or disagreement. [U. p12]

2.14   **True.** It is suitable for person-oriented tasks. [U. p15]

2.15   **False.** While Broadbent described an early selection theory, the above describes the process hypothesised in late selection. In early selection, most sensory information is lost early on in processing. [FF. p44–5]

2.16   **True.** [LL. p142–4]

2.17   **False.** The belief that is held with less conviction is the one that changes. [M. p18]

2.18   **True.** [A. p19]

2.19   **False.** He considered it to be 'polymorphously perverse', i.e.

sexual excitation could occur from several sources as a result of its component instincts. **[I. p574]**

2.20   **False.** The theory attempts to explain the experiences associated with empathy. **[G. p244]**

2.21   **False.** Chomsky proposes that the language acquisition device develops independently of non-linguistic cognitive processes. **[FF. p75]**

2.22   **True. [EE. pA–12]**

2.23   **True.** Fodor (1982) suggested that the sufferer may be discontented with the role of housewife but is unable to reject it overtly. **[FF. p218]**

2.24   **False.** They are not dyadic. **[LL. p37–8]**

2.25   **True.** Seligman 1971. **[A. p27]**

2.26   **True. [LL. p105]**

2.27   **False.** This is the ability to undo mentally an operation that was carried out before, and does not develop until the concrete operational stage. **[G. p137]**

2.28   **True.** He considered the sexual drive to be the more important drive. **[JJ. p76]**

2.29   **True. [W. p242]**

2.30   **True.** In standard, coloured and advanced versions. **[A. p38]**

2.31   **False.** For her, it was a serious consequence of neurotic development, leading to repression of emotions and genuine thoughts. **[I. p630]**

2.32   **False. [FF. p73–5]**

2.33   **True. [I. p396]**

2.34   **False.** The object relationship determines the libidinal attitudes. **[JJ. p128]**

2.35   **False.** This is the correlation for identical twins reared together; 0.70 is closer for those reared apart. **[EE. p479]**

2.36   **False.** They are the characteristic of 'insight' learning. **[EE. p281]**

2.37   **True. [EE. p761]**

2.38   **False.** The child is capable of this around the age of 3–4 years. **[LL. p33]**

2.39   **True. [M. p14]**

2.40   **False.** Attachment seems to persist in spite of these adversities. **[LL. p66–7]**

2.41   **False.** Berry (1991) showed that only when the subject actively participates in such a task would it facilitate performance. **[FF. p37]**

2.42   **True. [A. p17]**

2.43   **False.** Fading. **[A. p28]**

2.44   **True. [LL. p16]**

2.45   **True. [U. p71]**

2.46   **False.** It has a capacity of seven chunks. **[G. p378]**

2.47   **False.** An intrinsic motivation theory, since it does not involve reducing drives externally. **[U. p8]**

2.48   **True. [EE. p761]**

2.49   **False.** No such law. Gestalt psychology describes a number of 'laws' relating to perceptual phenomena: the laws of simplicity, closure, continuity, similarity and proximity. It also describes the fact that whole perception is different than the sum of its parts and 'figure ground discrimination'. **[U. p4]**

2.50   **False.** They are found to develop delayed grief. **[LL. p270]**

2.51   **False.** Children and males. **[H. p42]**

2.52   **True. [Q. p95–6]**

2.53   **True.** Also known as alcoholic blackouts. **[H. p51]**

2.54   **False.** Over-activity is not a characteristic feature. **[Q. p89]**

2.55   **True.** Along with impaired insight, personality distortion and impaired reality testing. **[Q. p10]**

2.56   **False.** The individual can be a healthy habitual hyposomniac. **[NN. p1395]**

2.57   **False.** The first two subdivisions are correct; the last is the 'motility psychosis', which may take hyperkinetic or akinetic forms. **[Q. p12]**

2.58   **True. [NN. p1741]**

2.59   **False.** They cannot be changed much by will alone. **[X. p4]**

2.60   **True.** His other fundamental symptoms are his '4 As' and disturbances of volition and behaviour. **[F. p76]**

2.61   **True.** It is an exaggerated form of mitmachen whereby only a slight push to the patient will send him off in a direction despite his being asked to resist this. **[V. p15]**

2.62   **True. [B. p437]**

2.63   **False.** No, it means 'depending on others'. **[I. p679]**

2.64   **True.** Conflict within the ego is what one would like to be and what one is. **[NN. p1118]**

2.65   **False.** A primary delusional experience. **[Q. p40]**

2.66   **True. [Q. p16]**

2.67   **False.** Katathymic amnesia. **[Q. p59]**

2.68   **True. [Q. p85]**

2.69   **True. [H. p56]**

2.70   **False.** The real change is in mood, which may lead on to delusion.

[X. p12]

2.71   **False.** Just four criminals. [H. p60]

2.72   **False.** The essence of social therapy is authoritarian structure, openness and shared examination of problems. [J. p151–3]

2.73   **True.** [H. p85]

2.74   **False.** This term refers to a schizophrenic's incongruent behaviour contradicting his beliefs. [X. p10]

2.75   **True.** [Q. p32]

2.76   **True.** [J. p177]

2.77   **False.** In contrast to amnesia resulting from diencephalic lesions, insight tends to be retained. [H. p52]

2.78   **True.** [Q. p63]

2.79   **False.** Objects are seen as being bigger on one side than on the other. [H. p79]

2.80   **False.** Hoenig disputed Money and Hampsons' finding. [J. p43]

2.81   **False.** Both are experienced as being clear and sharp but pseudo-hallucinations lack the sense of substance that hallucinations have. [Q. p19]

2.82   **True.** [Q. p99]

2.83   **False.** He saw them as being different from 'normal' only in degree. [Q. p10]

2.84   **True.** [Q. p21]

2.85   **False.** Cataplexy is sudden loss of muscle tone, often associated with emotion. [F. p16]

2.86   **True.** Hence it is also called as jargon aphasia. [B. p284]

2.87   **True.** [H. p66]

2.88   **False.** As they have true hypoacusis. [Q. p15]

2.89   **True.** In contrast to metonymy where a related word to the idea is used in an unusual way. Note that this is contradicted by Fish's description! [I. p688]

2.90   **False.** This is negative autoscopy. [Q. p27]

2.91   **False.** The reverse is true. The incorporation of delusions into more elaborate systems requires a more intact personality structure, according to Fish/Hamilton, which is affected more in those who develop schizophrenia when young. [Q. p42]

2.92   **False.** Other imageries such as pareidolia can. [X. p3]

2.93   **True.** [H. p326]

2.94   **True.** [Q. p49]

2.95   **False.** Snaith and Taylor describe this; Tyrer considers irritability to be a symptom of anxiety. [H. p300]

2.96   **True.** [J. p89]

2.97 **True.** [Q. p22]

2.98 **False.** These are acceptable behaviours. [NN. p2165]

2.99 **False.** Dereistic thinking is characterised by excessive and meandering fantasy thinking. [Q. p34]

2.100 **False.** They are based on biological predispositions. [NN. p1430–1]

2.101 **True.** Also increased serotinergic transmission to the limbic system. [Y. p47]

2.102 **False.** Thioridazine causes mydriasis whereas chlorpromazine causes miosis. [X. p586]

2.103 **False.** It is an idiosyncratic reaction with an incidence of 1–3 per 100,000. Signs include: diminished alertness, jaundice, haemorrhage, ascites, oedema, nausea and vomiting. [I. p2295]

2.104 **True.** Though it crosses placental barrier, there is no positive evidence of teratogenicity. [OO. p147–8]

2.105 **True.** [E. p40]

2.106 **False.** Both endozepines and diazepam binding inhibitor (DBI) are identified in human brain tissue but their physiological roles remain doubtful. [II. p111]

2.107 **False.** Up to 38% is excreted in faeces. [I. p2330]

2.108 **False.** Bioequivalence is a function of plasma concentration. [II. p30]

2.109 **True.** However they are rare. [I. p2342]

2.110 **False.** It can impair memory function 18 hours after a single dose. [II. p42]

2.111 **True.** [Z. p114]

2.112 **True.** [II. p182]

2.113 **True.** [OO. p157]

2.114 **False.** Fluoxetine can cause hyperglycaemia on discontinuation of treatment. [II. p176]

2.115 **False.** Only about 1.5–3 hours. [T. p329]

2.116 **True.** This is a potassium sparing diuretic. [II. p210]

2.117 **True.** As many as half of patients may get a degree of this. [OO. p140]

2.118 **False.** In zero-order kinetics, the drug concentration is independent of the processes of absorption and elimination. [II. p29]

2.119 **False.** Another new 'atypical' antipsychotic agent that has little associated weight gain as one of its advantages. [S. p88]

2.120 **False.** The SSRIs' anti-obsessive effects are independent of their antidepressant effects. [II. p175]

2.121 False. Its metabolite does block dopamine, but it has relatively low anticholinergic properties compared with other tricyclics. **[E. p182]**

2.122 True. [NN. p1938]

2.123 True. While clonidine has been associated with causing depression, a few open trials have suggested some efficacy in mania. **[I. p2355]**

2.124 True. Benzodiazepine related mania and hypomania have been reported in patients with and without a history of bipolar affective disorder **[NN. p1939]**.

2.125 False. It is thought not to have muscle-relaxant properties as a result of its much higher affinity for BZ_1 receptors as opposed to BZ_2 receptors. **[I. p2322]**

2.126 False. They are reversibly and dynamically bound to peripheral sites from where they are readily released back into the systemic circulation as excretion progresses. **[B. p85]**

2.127 True. [Z. p126]

2.128 True. [NN. p1917]

2.129 True. [T. p514]

2.130 False. Only the risk of toxic effects is minimised. **[X. p562]**

2.131 False. It does not blockade dopamine receptors, rather it depletes presynaptic indolamine and catecholamine stores. **[E. p128]**

2.132 True. [II. p254]

2.133 False. Much longer: three days. **[S. p110]**

2.134 True. Trazodone lacks noradrenaline re-uptake blockade. **[NN. p2089]**

2.135 True. There is very little weight change associated with loxapine treatment. **[S. p92]**

2.136 False. It has two active metabolites which have antidepressant and dopamine receptor blockade effects. **[NN. p2099]**

2.137 False. A number of studies have shown β-adrenergic antagonists (most commonly propranolol) to be effective. **[E. p25]**

2.138 False. Loxapine lowers the seizure threshold and can cause epilepsy even in normal doses. **[OO. p135]**

2.139 True. [I. p1949]

2.140 True. This can occur in up to 30% of patients.

2.141 True. *Repeated Consumption of Grapefruit Juice Prolongs Triazolam Half-Life.* European Journal of Clinical Transplantation 2000; 56: 411–415.

2.142 False. Diazepam has relatively short duration of action. **[NN. p1935]**

2.143 False. It is also a result of their antihistamine activity. **[S. p44]**

2.144 False. Venlafaxine is associated with an increase in blood pressure. **[NN. p2121]**

2.145 True. About 19% will have developed it after four years of treatment. **[I. p2268]**

2.146 False. The therapeutic index is the ratio of minimum effective concentration and the maximum tolerated concentration. **[II. p40]**

2.147 False. It is not found in significant amounts in breast milk; neither are some of the tricyclic antidepressants such as clomipramine or dothiepin. **[I. p1949]**

2.148 True. [II. p208]

2.149 True. This is a test that can check for speech localisation before any areas of brain are resected in surgery. **[I. p2311]**

2.150 True. It is likely that the nature of secondary changes underlies the clinical efficacy of antidepressants. **[B. p102]**

2.151 False. This suggests that puerperal mania has less genetic input. **[C. p909]**

2.152 True. As does cyclothymic disorder. **[NN. p1068]**

2.153 True. [I. p1666]

2.154 False. A high prevalence of bipolar disorder. **[NN. p1085]**

2.155 False. It is higher in women with coronary artery disease. **[I. p1771]**

2.156 True. Patients tend to believe that they deserve punishment. **[NN. p1128]**

2.157 True. [I. p1743]

2.158 False. For the first time DSM-IV has included cultural considerations. **[NN. p905]**

2.159 True. However it may simply be a result of the insomnia of depression, rather than being the underlying sleep disturbance itself. **[A. p440]**

2.160 True. In a subdivision of section F4. **[X. p137]**

2.161 False. At least 50% will. **[I. p2266]**

2.162 True. [X. p171, 112 and 119]

2.163 False. However they are less common than persecutory delusions and auditory hallucinations. **[L. p86]**

2.164 False. 10% of asymptomatic cases present with dementia as the initial manifestation. **[NN. p1669]**

2.165 False. Plucking usually involves a number of different sites of body hair. **[I. p1706]**

2.166 False. Not in weight loss. **[NN. p1365]**

2.167 True. The range quoted is 11% to 23%. **[I. p1723]**
2.168 False. Methadone causes miosis. **[F. p48]**
2.169 False. P. S. F. Yip, A. Chao and C. W. F. Chiu. Seasonal variation in suicides: diminished or vanished. Experience from England and Wales, 1982–1996. British Journal of Psychiatry 2000; 177: 366–369. The authors note a diminishment in the traditional spring (and autumn for females) suicide peaks.
2.170 False. [B. p294]
2.171 True. [X. p172]
2.172 True. [B. p324]
2.173 False. It can of course be use for depressive episodes occurring during the course of schizophrenia, but it has not been shown to have any marked effects on negative symptoms. **[C. p223]**
2.174 False. This assumption is purely based on the self-reports of the population studied. **[B. p335]**
2.175 False. A meta-analysis of 18 studies showed improvements in cardiac adverse events and mortality at one year in the treatments reducing type A behaviour. **[I. p1771]**
2.176 True. The duration required for the diagnosis is 6 months. **[B. p372]**
2.177 True. This is still a contentious issue however. **[N. p117]**
2.178 False. Attacks are invariable in situational bound type. **[NN. p1196]**
2.179 False. Typically, a sudden onset. **[HH. p337]**
2.180 False. This indicates several disorders; the focus of fear indicates the diagnosis. **[NN. p1200]**
2.181 True. Thus reinforcing the link between low CSF 5-HIAA levels and impulse dyscontrol. **[I. p1666]**
2.182 False. This can be another reverse sign in a depressive disorder. **[NN. p1131]**
2.183 False. It predicts a good response. **[C. p222]**
2.184 False. Only during prefrontal functional activities. **[NN. p923]**
2.185 False. The reverse. Up to 30% of patients with Alzheimer's disease will have misidentification phenomena at some point over the course of the illness. **[N. p52]**
2.186 False. Anxiety and depressive symptoms are the common morbidities. **[NN. p785]**
2.187 True. R. Yehuda, L. Bierer, J. Schmeidler, D. H. Aferiat et al. Low Cortisol and Risk of PTSD in Adult Offspring of Holocaust Survivors. American Journal of Psychiatry 2000; 157(8): 1252–1259. Children of Holocaust survivors were studied; they had

lower levels of cortisol than controls irrespective of whether they
ever had PTSD themselves.

2.188 **True.** They often live with their family and believe that family
members would be of much help. **[NN. p848]**

2.189 **False.** The (biological) relatives of female probands are more at
risk than the relatives of male probands. **[I. p1745]**

2.190 **True. [NN. p1311]**

2.191 **True.** The 'distinct' or 'special' quality. **[A. p428]**

2.192 **False.** This is a panic disorder. **[X. p144]**

2.193 **True. [I. p1441]**

2.194 **False.** It was Richard Morton who first described the patients but
Gull first used this term. **[NN. p1361]**

2.195 **False.** Studies vary with some showing a slight male excess, others
showing roughly equal prevalence. **[X. p171]**

2.196 **False.** They are not described as maladaptive. The causal link to
stress has not been described. **[NN. p1420]**

2.197 **True.** Associated psychiatric disturbances and the widespread
physical symptoms can make the distinction difficult.

2.198 **False.** They both have increased apolipoprotein E4 factor. **[B.
p301]**

2.199 **True. [I. p1360]**

2.200 **True. [X. p322]**

Answers Three

3.1 **False.** It is the belief that the group to which one belongs is being treated unfairly in comparison to other groups. **[G. p233]**

3.2 **True.** Fixation in the anal expulsive stage may lead to these behaviour patterns. **[JJ. p101–3]**

3.3 **False.** They see themselves as more heterogeneous while those in another group are seen as more homogenous. **[M. p25]**

3.4 **True. [MM. p94]**

3.5 **True.** The terms refer to the individual's development of thought processes of its being a distinct individual. **[K. p58]**

3.6 **False.** This research focuses on intra-individual stability and inter-individual variability. **[JJ. p187]**

3.7 **True. [I. p567]**

3.8 **False.** He has cautioned against this attitude. **[MM. p117]**

3.9 **False.** This is true of children functioning at the preoperational stage. An example would be if the child correctly counts that there are five sheep and three cows and that there are eight animals when added together but then answers incorrectly when asked if there are more sheep than animals altogether i.e. the child cannot compare mentally a superclass with subclasses. **[FF. p6]**

3.10 **True. [MM. p30–31]**

3.11 **True. [FF. p91]**

3.12 **False.** Vice-versa. **[JJ. p182]**

3.13 **False.** The shadow is a universal complex that is associated with the ego. The reverse of the 'persona', it contains traits that are unacceptable to the individual irrespective of whether they are positive or negative traits. **[I. p622]**

3.14 **False.** Personality disorder is associated with his level 2. **[JJ. p132–3]**

3.15 **True. [U. p73]**

3.16 **False.** There is no support for this hypothesis. **[JJ. p164]**

3.17 **False.** It is a secondary emotion; that is, it is a combination of two primary emotions: anticipation and joy. **[M. p13]**

3.18 **False.** The drive to seek more affiliations diminishes after a few close affiliations. **[JJ. p139–40]**

3.19 True. [J. p40]

3.20 False. Married people remaining in a chronically confrontational relationship would be worse off. [FF. p264]

3.21 True. [K. p30]

3.22 False. This is a test for implicit memory. [FF. p101]

3.23 False. Wilhelm Reich described this. [I. p627]

3.24 True. [JJ. p303]

3.25 True. [I. p621]

3.26 True. [JJ. p421]

3.27 False. The child develops depth perception between three to six months, but will probably only be able to crawl well enough for the experiment at seven months! [EE. p195]

3.28 False. He emphasises the mediation of cognitive factors. [JJ. p440–1]

3.29 True. [EE. p548]

3.30 False. It is three way bi-directional influences of those variables. [JJ. p345]

3.31 True. [M. p1]

3.32 False. They become less retrievable with time. [EE. p309–10]

3.33 False. It refers more to the process whereby the patient's relatives, through the doctor, have the patient committed. [U. p78]

3.34 True. [JJ. p211–4]

3.35 True. [FF. p23]

3.36 False. His model is hierarchial. [JJ. p201]

3.37 False. It is another term for classical conditioning. Operant learning is sometimes known as 'instrumental learning'. [A. p24]

3.38 True. [MM. p17]

3.39 True. [A. p30]

3.40 False. The opposite is true. [EE. p365]

3.41 False. This describes 'marital skew'; schism refers to conflict between the parents leading to difficulties in allegiance for the child. [U. p74]

3.42 False. It rejects the concept of aggression having drive-like properties. [EE. p441]

3.43 True. [U. p10]

3.44 False. No such differences have been established. [EE. p402]

3.45 False. Typically four year olds. [FF. p16]

3.46 True. [EE. p556]

3.47 False. The 'shadowing' experiment. The familiarity of the nursery rhyme means that the individual can turn more of his or her attention to the other message. [A. p29]

3.48 **False.** Some Q items use less or more than nine piles. **[EE. p553]**

3.49 **True. [I. p426]**

3.50 **False.** Proactive interference. **[G. p388]**

3.51 **False.** By Sifneos in 1972. **[H. p281]**

3.52 **True. [NN. p1121]**

3.53 **False.** It refers to the delirious patient who mimes the actions that are normally associated with his job. **[Q. p84]**

3.54 **False.** He described this condition as not having a perceptual disorder. **[B. p431]**

3.55 **False.** The other end: the head. **[I. p680]**

3.56 **False.** In contrast to schizophrenic flattened affect, depressed patients experience this as painful. **[NN. p1127]**

3.57 **True.** It is somewhat analogous to dream work. **[Q. p42]**

3.58 **False.** This is not a defence mechanism; it means fragmentation of mental functioning. **[NN. p903]**

3.59 **False.** Bleuler described this as a form of schizophrenia in which the disturbance of speech is the main feature. **[Q. p54]**

3.60 **True. [NN. p1289]**

3.61 **True. [H. p54]**

3.62 **False.** Whatever the conditions depersonalisation occurs in, reality testing remains intact. **[NN. p1290]**

3.63 **False.** It is well preserved in hypnotised individuals. **[H. p66]**

3.64 **True. [NN. p1282]**

3.65 **False.** It can occur in normal individuals in certain situations, for example, getting 'shivers' up your spine on hearing a well-preformed piece of music. **[H. p27]**

3.66 **True. [B. p371]**

3.67 **True. [H. p33]**

3.68 **False.** Sometimes this is possible. **[Q. p17]**

3.69 **True. [H. p300]**

3.70 **False.** This is a nihilistic delusion. **[Q. p47]**

3.71 **False.** Only for one aspect of what the term 'micropsia' can signify, that is the experience that objects are retreating from the viewer but retaining their size. **[Q. p16]**

3.72 **False.** This is the use of psychological means such as hypnosis and/or explanation to prepare for labour, but only 5–10% of patients will get this marked degree of pain relief. **[H. p265]**

3.73 **True.** Many individuals will steadfastly report they have experienced the stimulus the experimenter stated would occur even when no such stimulus has been presented. **[Q. p20]**

3.74 **False.** Compulsive behaviour relieves the anxiety. **[X. p169–70]**

3.75   **True.** They occur in deep sleep, early in the night. **[H. p42]**

3.76   **True. [B. p316]**

3.77   **False.** It is closely connected with memory however; it denotes the sense of familiarity one has when previously memorised material is recalled into consciousness in response to a cue. **[H. p50]**

3.78   **False.** It could happen during manic excitement. **[X. p203]**

3.79   **False.** *Witzelsucht* is a silly, joking form of good humour more associated with frontal lobe syndromes. **[Q. p9]**

3.80   **False.** Although the fundamental symptoms are the result of psychoanalytical concepts, it was Manfred's father Eugen Bleuler who proposed fundamental symptoms. **[X. p281]**

3.81   **True. [H. p341]**

3.82   **False.** Speech confusion is another name for word salad. **[U. p85]**

3.83   **False.** *Vorbeigehen* is talking past the point. **[U. p85]**

3.84   **True. [U. p89–90]**

3.85   **False.** It is part of the definition of delusional perception that the meaning that a patient attributes to an object or situation cannot be seen as arising from his/her mood state. **[Q. p40]**

3.86   **True. [U. p95–6]**

3.87   **False.** The early stages, it usually disappears as intellectual functioning deteriorates. **[H. p54]**

3.88   **True.** This is the process that revises the dream content after wakening to comply with the rules of secondary process. **[U. p97]**

3.89   **True.** They are described as 'relational' functions. **[H. p34]**

3.90   **False.** Jung extended Freud's concept of libido beyond the sexual aspect of life to include every manifestations of mind. **[U.]**

3.91   **False.** It refers to causes that are not permanent such as those resulting from ingested substances. It is mainly a legal concept. **[H. p323]**

3.92   **False.** Persecutory ideation in personality disorders but not persecutory delusions themselves can be explained adequately by Freud's theory of projection. **[X. p15]**

3.93   **True. [H. p303]**

3.94   **False.** A child creates the 'false self' as a reaction to this pathological mothering. **[U. p103]**

3.95   **False.** Higher in the summer months. **[H. p71]**

3.96   **True.** Though the person may be puzzled about their ideas, resistance is not a feature of delusional mood; this resistance is more a feature of obsessions. **[X. p15]**

3.97   **True. [H. p82]**

3.98 **False.** Retrospective falsification is the adding in of false details to a normal memory recollection, whereas in confabulation, a completely false memory is added to fill the memory gaps. **[U. p91, X. p22]**

3.99 **False.** They are sensory deceptions. **[Q. p17]**

3.100 **True.** Subjectively the patient feels better but objectively symptoms persist. **[B. p94]**

3.101 **True.** 9-Hydroxyrisperidone. **[S. p102]**

3.102 **False. [II. p170]**

3.103 **False.** This would work in the opposite direction of the desired initial effect of decreasing dopamine transmission. **[S. p37]**

3.104 **True.** As lorazepam, a high potency benzodiazepine, has a short half-life. **[X. p543]**

3.105 **True.** Hence females may be treatable with lower doses than males. **[S. p82]**

3.106 **True. [X. p581]**

3.107 **False.** Only 5%. **[I. p2456]**

3.108 **True.** With reference to diphenhydramine. **[B. p102]**

3.109 **False.** CYP 3A4 metabolises it to an inactive metabolite, while CYP 2D6 produces an active form: O-desmethylvenlafaxine. **[I. p2428]**

3.110 **False.** Even though the preference for MAO types is true, these differences do not translate into anything clinically meaningful. **[B. p108]**

3.111 **True.** They tend to be perceived as being stronger tablets than tablets of intermediate size. **[Z. p88]**

3.112 **False.** The clinician should avoid this as some drugs with long half-life (e.g. diazepam) have relatively short duration of action. **[NN. p1934]**

3.113 **True. [I. p2391]**

3.114 **False.** All tricyclics have weak affinity for D_2 (dopamine) receptors. Clomipramine, trimipramine and amoxapine are the most potent tricyclics at D_2 receptor sites. **[B. p102]**

3.115 **False.** Possibly because of its lower affinity for peripheral α_1-adrenergic receptors. **[I. p2416]**

3.116 **False.** Alprazolam is associated with inter-dose rebound anxiety. **[NN. p1942]**

3.117 **True. [I. p2420]**

3.118 **False.** Lithium should be discontinued 24–48 hours before surgery. **[II. p213]**

3.119 **False.** The usual dose is 500–2000 mg, while the lethal dose is in the region of 5000–10,000 mg. **[E. p86]**

3.120 False. As there is no cardiotoxic effect and it is relatively safe in overdose. [**II. p182**]

3.121 True. It is thought to inhibit the release of glutamate and aspartate from the presynaptic neuron and to reduce the entry of calcium into cells. [**I. p2301**]

3.122 False. There is a delay in absorption with slow release preparations resulting in reduced bioavailability which may be of some benefit in cases of overdose. [**II. p194**]

3.123 True. It is, however only on a named patient basis. [**OO. p89**]

3.124 True. [**II. p305–307**]

3.125 False. All three monoamines' reuptake is inhibited at high doses. [**Y. p63**]

3.126 False. Neurotoxicity can occur in about 10% of cases even when both drugs are within normal therapeutic ranges. [**II. p211–216**]

3.127 True. [**I. p2372**]

3.128 False. α-flupenthixol antagonises both dopamine and serotonin receptors. [**II. p264**]

3.129 False. It does not have significant antipsychotic activity. [**I. p2376**]

3.130 True. One study has reported a high incidence of HLA-1338, DR-4, and DQW3 white blood cell antigens. [**NN. p1984**]

3.131 True. Lithium carbonate tends to produce increases in the white cell count, and this effect usually predominates over that of carbamazepine. [**E. p82**]

3.132 False. Oxypertine depletes the storage of catecholamines. [**II. p281**]

3.133 False. It blocks α_2 receptors which promotes noradrenaline and 5HT release. It also blocks $5HT_2$ and $5HT_3$ receptors postsynaptically. It has little effect on reuptake inhibition. [**Y. p70**]

3.134 False. Benperidol is more potent than haloperidol. [**NN. p1990**]

3.135 False. It has been reported to have adverse effects on fertility and sperm cells. [**T. p266**]

3.136 False. So far PET studies are able to visualise dopamine receptors in the human striatum but not in human cortex. [**NN. p1995**]

3.137 True. [**I. p2412**]

3.138 False. α-receptor antagonism unopposed by cholinergic stimulation may be the underlying mechanism. [**NN. p2009**]

3.139 True. [**I. p2363**]

3.140 False. It does, it reduces the intensity of relapses. [**OO. p100**]

3.141 False. [**OO. p92**]

3.142 False. Reserpine and tetrabenazine are the only antipsychotics that do not interact with D_2 receptors. [NN. p1997]

3.143 **True.** It also blocks histamine and $5HT_2$ receptors. [Y. p69]

3.144 **True.** Other rare side-effects of risperidone are nasal stuffiness, nausea, vomiting and anxiety. [NN. p2018]

3.145 **True.** Zolpidem is an imidazopyridine hypnotic. [T. p326]

3.146 **True.** [NN. p2102]

3.147 **False.** Phase II trials are those involving preliminary studies on small groups of human patients. [Z. p71]

3.148 **True.** Due to increased adipose tissue as a result of weight gain. [U. p163]

3.149 **False.** It tends to be much higher in obese patients as opposed to those of normal weight (up to 50% higher). [I. p2379]

3.150 **True.** Disulfiram can cause hypothyroidism. [V. p337]

3.151 **False.** By Money and Werlwas in 1976. [I. p1535]

3.152 **False.** There is no such thing as epileptic personality. [B. p317]

3.153 **True.** As well as the risk of relapse in patients with schizophrenia. [A. p445]

3.154 **False.** Apraxia is the main disabling symptom. [B. p295]

3.155 **True.** This requirement is not present in ICD-10.

3.156 **False.** [B. p351]

3.157 **True.** As do parkinsonian features. [N. p55]

3.158 **False.** Thought disorders equally occur in mania. [B. p377]

3.159 **False.** He described its onset as tending to occur between the fourth and sixth decades. [L. p83]

3.160 **True.** Frontal areas from the perceptual parts of the brain. [B. p384]

3.161 **False.** UK 700 Group. Cost-effectiveness of intensive v. standard case management for severe psychotic illness. UK 700 case management trial. British Journal of Psychiatry 2000; 320: 537–543. There were no clear benefits noted for these indices.

3.162 **False.** This has not yet been demonstrated so far. [B. p411]

3.163 **False.** 1 to 2%. [C. p236]

3.164 **False.** Only pathoplastic effect. [B. p371]

3.165 **True.** Described by Marks, it is more common in the elderly.

3.166 **False.** Though obsessions can occur in encephalitis lethargica, rumination is not typical of this condition. [B. p437, 488 and 503]

3.167 **False.** This may occur in normal grief processes; however, note that this has always been a very contentious MCQ topic. [I. p1975]

3.168 **True.** [NN. p1075]

3.169 **True.** One third fulfil criteria a month after the death. [I. p1978]

3.170 False. He says that endogenomorphic depression is distinct from neurotic depression, as it is autonomous to precipitating stress. **[NN. p1137]**

3.171 True. [C. p918]

3.172 False. This risk is the same. **[F. p62]**

3.173 False. It is classed under 'other neurotic disorders'. **[I. p1564]**

3.174 True. [NN. p939]

3.175 False. Rigidity and akinesia develop more frequently than tremor does. **[I. p2265]**

3.176 True. They may be as useful as GGT levels. **[I. p965]**

3.177 False. It is not prominent outside of Jewish or Christian cultures. **[A. p435]**

3.178 False. This causes depression. The loss in the outer boundaries causes schizophrenia. **[NN. p959]**

3.179 True. It runs in families and causes marked insomnia as its name suggests; it is associated with thalamic dementia. **[N. p82]**

3.180 False. Men have a greater risk of developing alcoholism than women do. **[NN. p769]**

3.181 False. Around 75% of patients with paraphrenia will have them. **[N. p149]**

3.182 True. [NN. p1284]

3.183 True. K. Hawton, L. Harriss, L. Appleby, E. Juszczak, et al. 'Effect of death of Diana, Princess of Wales on suicide and deliberate self-harm'. British Journal of Psychiatry 2000; 177: 463–466.

3.184 True. In dissociative trance disorder which is included in DSM-IV, in appendix-B. **[NN. p1290–1]**

3.185 False. Although many are either normal weight or slightly overweight, the figure for those who have been markedly overweight is about 10%. **[I. p1672]**

3.186 False. Slower. **[X. p127]**

3.187 False. It has been shown by some studies to increase the risk for the development of coronary artery disease, but not to increase the further risks of events in individuals who have established coronary artery problems. **[I. p1771]**

3.188 False. This occurs in delayed grief. **[X. p152]**

3.189 True. However it is higher in the postnatal period than it is during the pregnancy (both being lower than the risk for the general population). **[C. p918]**

3.190 False. His concept also includes illness behaviour as a result of a person's belief of being ill even if he is not suffering from actual physical illness. **[X. p147]**

3.191 **False.** They tend to be under-attentive to their children. **[I. p1537]**

3.192 **False.** This is a type of thought echo. **[Q. p23]**

3.193 **False.** Some authorities recommend their use to counteract the muscle rigidity. **[I. p2267]**

3.194 **False.** Kahlbaum also thought of catatonia as organic signs. **[Q. p86]**

3.195 **True.** The range given is 5–15%. **[HH. p337]**

3.196 **False.** The message, or logic, can be repeated in different words; this is echologia. **[Q. p100]**

3.197 **False.** One of the major differences is that Kraepelin included unipolar depression in the manic-depressive insanity category. **[A. p430]**

3.198 **False.** Delusional misinterpretation is secondary to persecutory delusions whereas delusional perception is a primary delusion. **[Q. p40]**

3.199 **True.** One of the reasons why MAOIs are contraindicated during pregnancy; impairment of foetal growth has been demonstrated in animal experiments. **[I. p1949]**

3.200 **False.** They also include the spouse. **[Q. p64]**

Answers Four

4.1 **False.** The subject learns to avoid the unpleasant stimulus altogether in the latter, while he learns to get away from the stimulus quickly once it starts to experience it in the former. **[A. p25]**

4.2 **False.** The differences were obvious in boys. **[EE. p103]**

4.3 **True.** **[U. p23]**

4.4 **False.** Thorndike's experiments were conducted on cats. **[EE. p266]**

4.5 **False.** 5–10 central dispositions. A cardinal disposition is one that dominates virtually all aspects of a person's life. **[EE. p528]**

4.6 **True.** This is one of the four characteristic features of instinctive behaviour. **[EE. p408]**

4.7 **False.** True except for the last bit: the 'adapted child' should replace the child-next-door. **[I. p636]**

4.8 **True. [EE. p525–6]**

4.9 **True. [I. p389]**

4.10 **False.** The correlation is only about 0.16. **[EE. p568]**

4.11 **True.** Social loafing occurs when an individual works less hard in a group than when alone. **[G. p256]**

4.12 **False.** Therapy is mostly conducted in a group setting. **[EE. p689]**

4.13 **False.** This was the suggestion of Rachman (1978). **[A. p27]**

4.14 **True. [EE. p580]**

4.15 **False.** Kohlberg believed that formal operational thought was necessary for the higher stages of moral reasoning. **[EE. p90]**

4.16 **False.** They can serve as an attachment figure to a younger sibling. **[LL. p47]**

4.17 **True. [U. p19]**

4.18 **False.** Both patterns correspond to their infant's secure attachment. **[LL. p131]**

4.19 **True. [U. p13]**

4.20 **False.** They are the key features of sixth stage of moral development. **[G. p178]**

4.21 **False.** The reverse is true. **[I. p482]**

4.22 **True. [U. p45]**

4.23   **True. [U. p70]**

4.24   **False.** According to Rachman, phobia can develop even by reading. **[A. p27]**

4.25   **True. [FF. p43]**

4.26   **True.** 'Das Ich' is the ego. **[JJ. p83–4]**

4.27   **False.** Although emotional over-involvement in the form of over-protection, for example, is associated with relapse, warmth and positive remarks was not found to predict relapse. **[U. p74]**

4.28   **False.** This concept is called 'linguistic relativism'. **[FF. p75–6]**

4.29   **False.** Lacan did. Like most of his work, it is a complex notion that in part draws on linguistic ideas. **[K. p65]**

4.30   **True. [G. p274]**

4.31   **True.** Escape conditioning is the form of aversive conditioning that is most resistant to extinction. **[M. p3]**

4.32   **False.** Vaughen and Leff study of EE also suggests that this factor is associated with poor outcome in depression. **[FF. p252]**

4.33   **True.** Especially in those who have previous psychotic episodes during their lifetime. **[M. p65]**

4.34   **False.** Also they didn't complete their course on time. **[JJ. p121]**

4.35   **False.** Boys are generally better at this. **[G. p190]**

4.36   **True.** But it is a necessary condition for effective therapy. **[JJ. p160–1]**

4.37   **True. [U. p7]**

4.38   **True.** Many of the descriptive adjectives used are synonymous. **[JJ. p180]**

4.39   **False.** Their fear responses are modified and diminished in strange environments. **[I. p1770]**

4.40   **True. [MM. p35–6]**

4.41   **False.** This is 'angry aggression'. Instrumental aggression has increased standing in society as its reinforcement. **[I. p1723]**

4.42   **True. [MM. p39]**

4.43   **True.** Four main different temperaments are described: novelty seeking, harm avoidance, reward dependence and persistence. **[I. p1724]**

4.44   **False.** They are three basic body types. His temperament types are viscerotonia, somatotonia and cerebrotonia. **[JJ. p229–30]**

4.45   **True.** Along with self-directedness and cooperativeness. **[I. p1730]**

4.46   **False.** After the learning has faded he may engage in that behaviour. **[JJ. p345]**

4.47   **False.** Hanscarl Leuner (1954). **[I. p2212]**

4.48 **False.** High frequency behaviours need not be pleasurable. **[JJ. p371]**

4.49 **True.** An end-product in noradrenaline metabolism. **[I. p1728]**

4.50 **True.** They are deficit and growth motivations. **[JJ. p417–9]**

4.51 **True.** A greater intensity of stimulus is required for all stimuli to reach consciousness in delirious states. **[Q. p15]**

4.52 **False.** This is a denial mechanism. **[JJ. p412]**

4.53 **True. [H. p33]**

4.54 **False.** More complex: it is an example of id and superego versus ego conflict. **[JJ. p86]**

4.55 **False.** Sims considers irritability to probably have an inverse relationship with age. **[H. p306]**

4.56 **True.** Harry Stack Sullivan uses this phrase to refer to the feelings of 'specialness'. **[JJ. p127–8]**

4.57 **False.** It is rare; it denotes the experience whereby the normal links between perceptions in different modalities are not made, for example not appreciating that the perceptions of seeing an approaching car and hearing its engine, are coming from the same source. **[H. p80]**

4.58 **False.** It is a simple form of classical conditioning. **[G. p119]**

4.59 **True.** That is, the patient believes that others with similar sensory acuity would not be able to perceive the hallucination, in contrast to real perceptions. **[H. p84]**

4.60 **False.** This means undirected fantasy thinking. **[Q. p34]**

4.61 **True.** If refers to the diminished reactivity of mood that can occur in depression whereby the individual does not have the same emotional response to stimuli that would normally cause such a response. **[Q. p79]**

4.62 **True. [Q. p69]**

4.63 **False.** It denotes the use of one word to signify a number of different meanings by the patient and may indeed be seen in schizophrenia. **[I. p683]**

4.64 **False.** Anxiety is not invariably present, according to the quoted text. **[X. p19]**

4.65 **True. [H. p79]**

4.66 **False.** Chronic inmates of an institution feel safe in spite of frequent changes in the staff. **[J. p60–1]**

4.67 **True. [I. p683]**

4.68 **False.** Artist Vincent van Gogh was predisposed to depression from a life event before his birth since he was named by his mother after a previous stillborn sibling; this had a major impact on him throughout his life. See reference for further details. [NN. p1556–9]

4.69   **True.** Individuals waking in the morning can wake and doze several times before waking fully. [Q. p21]

4.70   **False.** They become less materialistically concerned. [NN. p1716]

4.71   **False.** This is a description of pica. Polyphagia is simply abnormal overeating. [I. p686]

4.72   **True.** Zeigler and Sours thought so. [NN. p1361–2]

4.73   **False.** Sleepiness occurs in the absorption of transcendental meditation; it need not occur in trance. [H. p38]

4.74   **True.** They are hallucinogens. [F. p62]

4.75   **False.** Jaspers wrote it. [Q. p1]

4.76   **False.** Liposwski has cautioned about misdiagnosis of this state as depression. [B. p286–7]

4.77   **True.** Fish describes the voice pattern as 'strangled'. [Q. p99]

4.78   **False.** [B.296]

4.79   **False.** They are rare even in severe depression. [Q. p22]

4.80   **True.** [B. p341]

4.81   **True.** [Q. p32]

4.82   **False.** The fact that expressed emotions are less evident in the first episode of schizophrenia support this view. [B. p384]

4.83   **True.** [H. p294]

4.84   **True.** [B. p403]

4.85   **True.** They tend to retain exhibitionism as their deviation in a stable fashion. [H. p251]

4.86   **False.** They are only quantitatively different. [NN. p1215]

4.87   **True.** However, only in a subset of cases. [H. p251]

4.88   **True.** But a full panic attack will indicate agoraphobia with panic disorder. [NN. p1197]

4.89   **False.** A discrepancy of five years. [Q. p66]

4.90   **True.** From anomalous experiences that demand explanations. [NN. p1040]

4.91   **False.** They tend to be unperturbed by this, or by not being able to tell the direction from which the voices are coming. [Q. p22]

4.92   **False.** They do not occur in middle cerebral artery embolism but can occur in posterior cerebral artery embolism. [NN. p182]

4.93   **False.** Autoscopy involves only the sense of vision. [H. p95]

4.94   **True.** [NN. p1288]

4.95   **True.** Particularly with the fear of ageing. [H. p228]

4.96   **False.** Emotion reducing strategies are not always healthy (e.g. alcohol). [X. p135]

4.97 **True.** However, it is more usual that the individual thinks that the penis is retracting into the abdomen. **[H. p123]**

4.98 **False.** Denial is a defence mechanism. The common coping strategy is avoidance. **[X. p139]**

4.99 **True.** That is, they are not of major importance in themselves, rather they are by-products of the brain's essential functions.

4.100 **False.** It is a disorder of mood. **[Q. p9]**

4.101 **False.** Significant prolongation of the QT interval may produce this. The normal QT interval is usually less than 450–500 ms. **[S. p86]**

4.102 **False.** They do not interact with β-blockers. **[X. p564]**

4.103 **True.** It also has marked EPSE in high doses. **[S. p75]**

4.104 **True. [II. p217]**

4.105 **False.** It is about 35% bound. **[I. p2428]**

4.106 **True. [B. p92]**

4.107 **False.** It is less common in these patients. **[Z. p125]**

4.108 **False.** Tricyclic metabolism is not unidirectional; a secondary amine like desipramine could be converted to tertiary amine, imipramine. **[B. p101]**

4.109 **True.** Pimozide is an example of a diphenylbutylpiperidine. **[I. p2361]**

4.110 **True. [II. p290]**

4.111 **True.** However, this effect is rare. **[E. p83]**

4.112 **True.** Stale-blue pigmentation in exposed areas is termed 'oculodermal melanosis', as this is associated with ophthalmological changes. **[II. p293]**

4.113 **False.** Studies have found higher doses to be of benefit (up to and beyond 500 mg per day). Most studies however have been open in design. **[I. p2274]**

4.114 **False.** Chlorpromazine and flupenthixol but not fluphenazine are enzyme inducers. **[II. p294]**

4.115 **True. [I. p2318]**

4.116 **True. [E. p188]**

4.117 **False.** Since it is excreted into breast milk in large quantities, it is contraindicated for this purpose. **[OO. p148]**

4.118 **False.** They may offer possible explanations of therapeutic effect. Changes in neurophysins and evening cortisol may give better prediction of outcome. **[II. p242]**

4.119 **True.** Hence it is more sedating. **[Y. p66]**

4.120 **True.** These are uncommon side-effects **[II. p217]**

4.121 **True.** It is probable that case reports of some EPSE associated with it will come in due course, however at present it appears to be the agent with the least risk of EPSE. **[S. p82]**

4.122 False. Elderly patients are at much greater risk of death from agranulocytosis, but they are at no greater risk for agranulocytosis. **[NN. p1984]**

4.123 False. It is an antagonist of the benzodiazepines; an inverse agonist would cause the opposite effects of the benzodiazepines (such as increased anxiety, insomnia, sweating and so on). **[T. p321]**

4.124 False. Higher doses (100–250/day) may exacerbate the parkinsonian symptoms. **[NN. p1983]**

4.125 True. This is contentious, but this has been reported in at least one study. **[I. p2440]**

4.126 False. The psychopathology seems to be more related to neurodysfunction. **[II. p275]**

4.127 True. [Z. p91]

4.128 True. [NN. p1991]

4.129 False. About 15% is excreted by the gastrointestinal system. **[I. p2391]**

4.130 True. Prolactin levels return to normal within days. **[NN. p2009]**

4.131 False. At least 4%. **[I. p2386]**

4.132 False. Haloperidol and risperidone are the drugs of choice for cardiac patients because of low anticholinergic and adrenergic effects. **[NN. p2007]**

4.133 True. As is the anxiety and agitation associated with SSRI treatment. **[Y. p52]**

4.134 False. Only in 40% to 50% of cases. **[NN. p2004]**

4.135 True. It is metabolised by cholinesterase instead. **[I. p2351]**

4.136 False. This is an exception among the secondary amines, which has more sedative effects. **[NN. p2108]**

4.137 False. Because clomipramine has so much 5HT activity, it is contraindicated in patients on MAOIs. Trimipramine is the tricyclic that tends to be used in combination with MAOIs. **[Y. p33]**

4.138 False. Disulfiram is a potent cytochrome inhibitor. **[NN. pp450, 2110, 2125]**

4.139 True. It also has some activity in decreasing glutamate levels. **[T. p270]**

4.140 False. Intramuscular chlorpromazine (50–100 mg) can be used if phentolamine is not available. **[OO. p190]**

4.141 False. It has little or no analgesic properties. **[I. p2344]**

4.142 True. [II. p285]

4.143 False. 2–3 hours, hence the six-hourly dosing necessary. **[I. p2347]**

4.144 False. Despite its structural relationship to GABA, gabapentin is not a GABA mimetic. **[II. p346]**

4.145 True. [OO. p89]

4.146 False. Unlike the enzyme inducers, since they are enzyme inhibitors they do not reduce plasma levels of oestrogen. **[II. p350]**

4.147 False. It does this indirectly by first allosterically modulating the GABA A receptor-binding site, which then can affect the chloride channel. **[T. p317]**

4.148 True. Chronic forms of akathesia may have these characteristics **[II. p286]**

4.149 True. It has been used to reduce anxiety in OCD. **[E. p67]**

4.150 True. This is true with higher doses (above 20 mg daily) of fluoxetine. **[II. p176]**

4.151 True. [I. p2266]

4.152 False. Goldberg reported obsessive thoughts and mild compulsions in this disorder. **[X. p157]**

4.153 False. Intravenous anticholinergics are indicated such as benztropine. **[I. p2267]**

4.154 True. Such as compulsive licking and biting. **[NN. p1368]**

4.155 True. As well as in patients with schizophrenia. **[A. p441]**

4.156 False. It begins between the age of 4 years and 12 years: night terrors. **[NN. p1387]**

4.157 True. Primary depressions are those that are not preceded by any other psychiatric disorder (with the exception of a manic episode). **[A. p433]**

4.158 False. The monozygotic twin of a schizophrenic proband has a slightly more elevated risk than the children of two schizophrenic parents. **[F. p79]**

4.159 False. It is an assessment schedule for dementia. **[L. p137]**

4.160 True. [B. p293]

4.161 True. There are marked changes in white matter as a result of the progressive small vessel disease: it is another vascular dementia. **[N. p75]**

4.162 False. This is common in Alzheimer's disease. **[B. p300]**

4.163 True. Some studies have found much higher rates than this. **[N. p150]**

4.164 False. Euphoria is not that common (10%). **[B. p320]**

4.165 True. Also schizophrenia with delusional mood or persecutory delusions. **[C. p222]**

4.166 False. It has increased the service utilisation by the users. **[B. p332]**

4.167 False. Mulholland, C. and Cooper, S. The symptom of depression in schizophrenia and its management. Advances in Psychiatric Treatment 2000; vol. 6: p174. (Quoted from Addington *et al.* 1996).

4.168 True. Particularly the young offenders. **[B. p348]**

4.169 True. [C. p229]

4.170 True. [B. p305]

4.171 False. According to Kessler *et al.* the prevalence is 4% in males and 13% in females. **[X. p170]**

4.172 True. If the dialysis is too rapid. **[C. p1160]**

4.173 True. These occur when the bereaved person adopts traits or actions of the deceased. **[I. p1975]**

4.174 False. This association has not been recently confirmed. **[B. p317]**

4.175 False. One study has shown it to be higher in these patients; serotoninergic systems are thought to mediate satiety in the CNS. **[I. p1666]**

4.176 False. The most important diagnostic procedure is an in-depth interview. **[NN. p1373]**

4.177 False. This is the DSM-IV time criterion; ICD-10 requires that the symptoms start within one month of the stressor. **[GG]**

4.178 True. It is a change in one's perception of mental contents. **[NN. p1290]**

4.179 True. Women are more likely to report irritable bowel syndrome, functional constipation and globus. **[I. p1778]**

4.180 False. There is no definite time frame to diagnose this disorder. Rather this is based on subjective satisfaction of both partners. **[NN. p1309–10]**

4.181 False. Only about 50% have no medical condition to account for it; reflux of gastric acid accounts for most of the medically explained forms. **[I. p1776]**

4.182 True. The other abnormalities are: microcephaly, brain development defects, haemorrhagic lesions and placenta praevia. **[NN. p830]**

4.183 True. Sleep patterns are severely affected. **[C. p909]**

4.184 False. The symptoms will be more severe than the original symptoms. **[NN. p850]**

4.185 False. The diagnosis is not given to patients who admit their subterfuge easily. **[I. p1533]**

4.186 **True.** Also decreased amplitude of event related potentials. **[NN. p781]**

4.187 **False.** The jaw is affected. **[I. p2267]**

4.188 **True. [NN. p1345]**

4.189 **True. [A. p447]**

4.190 **False.** This condition is associated with panic attacks. **[NN. p1244]**

4.191 **True.** Under 'Other Mood Disorders': F38.10. **[A. p434]**

4.192 **False.** Women have higher levels. **[NN. p1078]**

4.193 **False.** The risk for relatives of probands with late-onset depression is at least half that for relative of probands with early-onset depression. **[N. p110]**

4.194 **True. [NN. p1145]**

4.195 **True. [N. p188]**

4.196 **True. [C. p1163]**

4.197 **False.** A. H. Crisp, M. G. Gelder, S. Rix, H. I. Meltzer et al. Stigmatisation of people with mental illnesses. British Journal of Psychiatry 2000; 177: 4–7. About 70% of people think this.

4.198 **False.** These also occur after partial sleep deprivation. **[B. p418]**

4.199 **True. [X. p166]**

4.200 **True. [B. p417]**

Answers Five

5.1   **True.** [A. p24]
5.2   **False.** New-borns can discriminate different odours and taste but they are short sighted at birth. [EE. p80]
5.3   **False.** *Laissez-faire* leadership is more appropriate for this. [U. p15]
5.4   **False.** The child has failed to achieve gender constancy. [EE. p105]
5.5   **False.** He emphasised an integrated model of biological, dynamic and social concerns. [I. p617]
5.6   **True.** [JJ. p257–8]
5.7   **True.** It is a form of cognitive mode of experience, coming after the 'prototaxic' mode and before the 'syntactic' one. [I. p634]
5.8   **False.** They both act interdependently upon each other. [FF. p143]
5.9   **True.** As seen in the 'learned helplessness' experiments. [EE. p274]
5.10 **False.** Newborn infants exhibit 'reflexive emotional resonance'. [B. p66]
5.11 **True.** As opposed to primary territories that are accessible to only a small number of people. [G. p270]
5.12 **True.** [FF. p162]
5.13 **False.** Greater skin resistance: Sternbach (1962). [FF. p145]
5.14 **True.** [JJ. p119–24]
5.15 **False.** Operant conditioning. [I. p417]
5.16 **False.** According to Garden, this can be viewed as a positive development. [JJ. p110]
5.17 **True.** Apart from the positive reinforcement of praise etc, the patient will typically have motives of wanting to get out of the aversive environment when he/she decides to comply with treatment. [I. p418]
5.18 **True.** [JJ. p194–5]
5.19 **False.** A logarithmic function. [U. p4]
5.20 **False.** The incidence of violence actually increases. [MM. p250]
5.21 **False.** However this ability develops very soon after birth, as does depth perception. [M. p7]

5.22 **False.** This has only three sources of data: L, T and Q data. **[JJ. p201]**

5.23 **True.** The unconditioned stimulus leads to an unconditioned response which, if combined with another stimulus by the individual, leads to this stimulus becoming the conditioned stimulus. Then stimulus generalisation and reinforcement act on this process. **[A. p27]**

5.24 **True. [EE. p168]**

5.25 **False.** Berscheid and Walster (1974) hypothesise that individuals tend to pair off with individuals with a similar level of attractiveness as themselves. **[U. p41]**

5.26 **True. [JJ. p323]**

5.27 **True. [I. p628]**

5.28 **True.** This is not an aversive procedure. **[JJ. p373]**

5.29 **False.** In their own interest. More elaborate theories have been developed to explain acts of altruism. **[I. p488]**

5.30 **False.** With the exception of Klahr, they agree with Piaget. **[EE. p94]**

5.31 **False.** This is true of children of *authoritarian* parents. **[EE. p800]**

5.32 **True. [EE. p331]**

5.33 **True.** Obviously discredited. The familial communications they proposed as being harmful did not proceed logically in terms of content as most communication is supposed to. **[M. p63]**

5.34 **False.** It uses the standard age scores. **[EE. p460]**

5.35 **False.** They develop this at about one month of age. **[M. p6]**

5.36 **True. [EE. p336]**

5.37 **True. [M. p7]**

5.38 **False.** It increases the subjective experience of that emotion. **[EE. p433]**

5.39 **False.** Goffman's description may appear to make this question less nonsensical than first impressions suggest. However, the concept involves an enclosed society with a rigid daily routine. **[U. p78]**

5.40 **True. [EE. p560]**

5.41 **False.** Splitting and projection. **[A. p88]**

5.42 **False.** She has the signal to relax safely. **[EE. p580]**

5.43 **True.** As opposed to 'top-down' processing, which is influenced by previous experiences, a more highly processed representation. **[I. p388]**

5.44 **False.** They are based on John Bowlby's attachment theory. **[LL. p20–21]**

5.45 **True. [EE. p351]**
5.46 **True. [LL. p187]**
5.47 **False.** This was Klein's view; Freud saw the newborn as being completely id. **[K. p56]**
5.48 **False.** Social class 0. **[U. p69]**
5.49 **True. [U. p22]**
5.50 **False.** The reverse is true. **[U. p2]**
5.51 **False.** This is true of a phobia. *'Prüfung'* is the German for an examination. **[Q. p68]**
5.52 **False.** This is an example of stereotypic posture. **[Q. p101]**
5.53 **False.** Noesis is the intense revelation a patient gets in which he understands that he is an appointed leader of people for some purpose. It is thus more associated with manic states. **[I. p685]**
5.54 **True. [J. p148]**
5.55 **True.** Grammar and syntax are unaffected but the continuity of the speech content is. **[Q. p51]**
5.56 **False.** A psychiatrist cannot distinguish this and hence warrants caution when assessing risk. **[Q. p75]**
5.57 **False.** This is 'fluent plausible lying' and is distinct from confabulation. It is associated with Munchausen's syndrome and personality disorders. **[H. p57]**
5.58 **True.** This is a passivity phenomenon. **[Q. p38]**
5.59 **True. [H. p310]**
5.60 **False.** The stages of Carl Jung. **[J. p39]**
5.61 **False.** Sensitivity is a common feature of anankastic traits. **[H. p311]**
5.62 **False.** They are secondary to disturbance of recall. **[Q. p61]**
5.63 **True. [H. p43]**
5.64 **False.** Flight of ideas is rare in elation found in schizophrenia and organic conditions. **[Q. p73]**
5.65 **True. [H. p45]**
5.66 **False. [Q. p37]**
5.67 **False.** Auditory hallucinations tend to be short utterances. **[Q. p20]**
5.68 **True. [X. p15]**
5.69 **False.** One can only empathise with experiences one has in common with others. **[Q. p2]**
5.70 **True. [J. p115]**
5.71 **False.** Unusually for a form of visual hallucination, the patient generally is pleased to witness them. **[Q. p25]**
5.72 **True. [H. p144]**

5.73 **True.** An individual experiences an autoscopic hallucination when one sees oneself in external space. **[X. p6]**

5.74 **False.** In mitmachen the part of the body moved returns to the resting position. **[Q. p97]**

5.75 **False.** Pareidolic illusions tend to become more distinct, the more one concentrates on them. **[H. p39]**

5.76 **False. [Q. p19]**

5.77 **False.** The original description stated that behaviour is relatively well organised. **[Q. p85]**

5.78 **True. [Q. p59]**

5.79 **True.** As opposed to delusion-like ideas. **[Q. p39]**

5.80 **False.** He used this term to describe depression with pre-cordial anxiety. **[Q. p71]**

5.81 **False.** It occurs when an individual recalls something and uses that memory without realising it as a memory; for example, replying with an answer that is a quote, but thinking that it is an original comment. **[H. p59]**

5.82 **False.** *Schnauzkrampf* occurs especially in catatonia. **[Q. p89]**

5.83 **True. [H. p53]**

5.84 **False.** It is both thought and motor blocking. **[Q. p90]**

5.85 **False.** They are characterised by sudden onset and offset. **[H. p32]**

5.86 **True. [U. p93]**

5.87 **False.** Reduced, hence the individual appears out of touch with what is going on around him. **[H. p38]**

5.88 **False. [Q. p79]**

5.89 **True.** Leading weight to the argument that a foetal insult may be important in aetiology for some individuals. **[H. p71]**

5.90 **True. [X. p191]**

5.91 **False.** This is unlikely, as sleepwalking tends to occur in the first third of sleep. **[H. p42]**

5.92 **True. [X. p191]**

5.93 **True. [H. p46]**

5.94 **False.** Though the influence is mutual, crucially it is the system's setting that influences the individual. **[J. p52]**

5.95 **True.** As are the patient's 'set' and how clearly they perceive their environment. **[Q. p17]**

5.96 **False. [U. p88]**

5.97 **False.** It differentiates hallucinations from mental images; pseudo-hallucinations are a type of mental image. **[Q. p19]**

5.98 **True. [X. p253]**

5.99 **True.** Apart from his work on physical pathology. **[Q. p5]**

5.100 False. Apraxia does not occur as a result of motor defects. **[PP. p55–8]**

5.101 False. 1A2 is induced, leading to larger doses of the drug being required (this is the same for clozapine). **[S. p86]**

5.102 False. MAO-B does not act on noradrenaline or serotonin. **[U. p168]**

5.103 True. However, the half-life of its active metabolite, *O*-desmethylvenlafaxine, is about 10 hours. **[I. p2428]**

5.104 True. Anecdotal reports suggest this in a patient receiving fluphenazine. **[NN. p2009]**

5.105 False. It is less sedating. **[Z. p118]**

5.106 True. [NN. p1997]

5.107 False. Since platelets contain MAO-B **[I. p2400]**

5.108 False. α-adrenergic agents but not β-adrenergic agonists are the drugs of choice as the latter can paradoxically worsen the antipsychotic-induced hypotension. **[NN. p2007]**

5.109 True. [I. p2368]

5.110 True. [NN. p1991]

5.111 False. Since it is an inhibitor of anticholinesterase, physostigmine may indeed be used to treat anticholinergic intoxication, but it can lead to severe hypotension and bronchial constriction. **[E. p38]**

5.112 True. They are broad-spectrum atypical antipsychotics. **[II. p269]**

5.113 True. [I. p2313]

5.114 True. [NN. p1994]

5.115 True. [I. p2280]

5.116 False. The opposite is true. **[II. p217]**

5.117 False. Although it has antidepressant properties in its own right, it is much less potent than fluoxetine in 5HT reuptake inhibition. **[OO. p116]**

5.118 False. Asymptomatic or non-progressive leucopenia does not warrant carbamazepine discontinuation. **[II. p216]**

5.119 True. There is one tricyclic depot preparation: imipramine pamoate. **[E. p182]**

5.120 False. These storage-depleting neuroleptics produce other extrapyramidal side-effects but do not produce tardive dyskinesia. **[II. p287]**

5.121 False. It however has little anticholinergic or antihistaminergic properties. **[S. p71]**

5.122 True. Due to an increased risk of severe neurotoxicity. **[II. p297]**

5.123 True. It has the lowest potential for blocking noradrenaline reuptake. **[I. p2435]**

5.124 False. There is no evidence for this and one study reported the opposite trend. **[II. p286]**

5.125 False. Raised plasma levels provide this support. **[Z. p104]**

5.126 True. [II. p301]

5.127 False. There is little evidence that moclobemide is especially useful for 'atypical' depression; indeed the evidence of this for classical MAOIs is not strong. **[I. p2402]**

5.128 True. Particularly some patients with epilepsy are more vulnerable to this. **[II. p212]**

5.129 False. Sexual dysfunction is part of their side-effect profile. **[Y. p32]**

5.130 False. It is recommended in patients with histories of these conditions as it has only weak anticholinergic properties. **[II. p183]**

5.131 True. However it does produce EPSE and hyperprolactinaemia comparable to haloperidol. **[S. p89]**

5.132 False. This anti-emetic is an exception in that it has apparently been shown to be teratogenic **[II. p317]**

5.133 True. As does rivastigmine. Tacrine inhibits both. **[T. p481]**

5.134 True. [II. p353]

5.135 False. It has the most marked antagonism in this order: $\mu > \delta > \kappa$. **[I. p2407]**

5.136 True. Tardive Tourette's Syndrome has been reported. **[II. p286–7]**

5.137 True. However, this is rare. **[I. p2385]**

5.138 True. This occurs in high serum anticonvulsant levels and in self-poisoning. **[II. p351]**

5.139 True. [E. p93]

5.140 False. This is a rare adverse effect. **[II. p357]**

5.141 False. One of the most noticeable aspects of paraldehyde use is the halitosis caused by excretion of unmetabolised drug via the lungs. The majority is metabolised however by the liver. **[I. p2314]**

5.142 False. Zopiclone produces fewer changes in sleep architecture. **[X. p547]**

5.143 True. One of the reasons that is put forward for the reduced incidence of extrapyramidal disorders with these agents. **[S. p52]**

5.144 False. Above 450 ng/ml may be cardiotoxic. **[NN. p1164]**

5.145 True. Other examples are pramiracetam and oxiracetam. **[T. p491]**

5.146 True. It interferes with the laboratory test for these. **[E. p199]**

5.147 False. Most commonly after the fifth day, but it may occur before this. **[I. p2368]**

5.148 False. This blocks the sexual side-effects of SSRIs. **[NN. p1315]**

5.149 True. Although recent evidence is conflicting, there is still some evidence that it causes less iatrogenic mania. **[I. p2327]**

5.150 False. Fluoxetine delays ejaculation. **[NN. p1315]**

5.151 False. About 30% in his study. **[X. p166]**

5.152 False. Major depression in general is associated with immuno-suppression. **[NN. p1566]**

5.153 False. It includes premenstrual tension but it does not provide a definition for it. **[I. p1953]**

5.154 True. [NN. p1563]

5.155 True. [I. p1770]

5.156 False. One person lives for the welfare of a significant person, neglecting his own life. **[NN. p1607]**

5.157 True. The acute separation response is associated with increased temperature and heart rate. **[I. p1769]**

5.158 False. Neither by hypnosis nor suggestion. **[NN. p1615]**

5.159 False. Some cases resolve directly to euthymia. **[C. p905]**

5.160 True. [J. p55]

5.161 True. However, this is not certain since there has been little research on the condition as a consequence of its rarity. **[I. p1550]**

5.162 False. Imaging studies have suggested the possibility of some permanent dysfunction. **[B. p415]**

5.163 False. It is not rare. **[A. p447]**

5.164 False. The specific diagnosis in which panic attack occurs is coded. **[NN. p1191]**

5.165 True. Although not all studies have confirmed this. **[L. p66]**

5.166 True. But they are not decreased in depression. **[B. p416]**

5.167 False. N. Seivewright and O. Lagundoye. What the clinician needs to know about magic mushrooms. *Advances in Psychiatric Treatment* 2000; vol. 6: 344–347. *Psilocybe semilanceata* is the commonest form of magic mushroom in Great Britain. It causes enlarged but reactive pupils.

5.168 True. As these depressions tend to be associated with a strong family history of bipolar disorders. **[NN. p1143]**

5.169 False. 1 in 22,000 treatments. **[C. p222]**

5.170 True. It is important to consider this possibility in mania developing in later life. **[NN. p1142]**

5.171 True. As are patients with borderline personality disorder. **[I. p1693]**

5.172 False. For meiosis and constipation the tolerance is less. **[NN.**

p846]
5.173 False. However, the act of stealing may be pleasurable to the individual. **[I. p1703]**
5.174 True. [NN. p804]
5.175 False. Over a half of cases in a 1961 study. **[C. p919]**
5.176 False. The Epidemiological Catchment Area study reported that only in some instances did the cocaine use antedate the psychiatric disorder. **[NN. p819]**
5.177 True. And commoner in middle age, however other factitious disorders tend to be commoner in females. **[I. p1536]**
5.178 False. Also studies on cerebral atrophy are controversial. **[NN. p813]**
5.179 False. About a quarter. **[A. p428]**
5.180 True. [NN. p248]
5.181 True. Objective depressive features predict shortened survival in Alzheimer's disease. **[N. p60]**
5.182 False. If there is loss of consciousness, posttraumatic headaches occur within 14 days after regaining consciousness. **[NN. p255]**
5.183 True. S. J. Leask, D. J. Done, T. J. Crow, M. Richards and P. B. Jones. No association between breast-feeding and adult psychosis in two national birth cohorts. British Journal of Psychiatry 2000; 177: 218–221. The quoted study however found no such evidence.
5.184 False. The second type is binge eating/purging type. **[NN. p1362]**
5.185 False. It is difficult to do a double-blind study of psychosurgery. **[C. p235]**
5.186 True. [NN. p1389]
5.187 True. Traditional community surveys may underreport the initial panic attack. **[X. p174]**
5.188 False. They have a lack of desire for social intimacy. **[NN. p1445]**
5.189 True. The commonest comorbid conditions however are depressive and anxiety disorders each occurring in about 65% of patients with anorexia nervosa according to the same study. **[I. p1665]**
5.190 True. [F. p31]
5.191 False. It is not included in the section of standard personality disorders; instead it is in the criteria sets for further study in the appendices. **[I. p1738]**
5.192 False. Nystagmus is unlikely to resolve. **[F. p72]**
5.193 True. [A. p428]
5.194 True. [B. p283]

5.195 False. It is part of the definition of the syndrome that the self-neglect does not have a psychiatric or medical illness sufficient to cause it. **[N. p166]**

5.196 True. [B. p334]

5.197 True. In other words, pseudohallucinations; insight as to their nature also tends to be preserved. **[I. p1556]**

5.198 True. When given by a trained person. **[B. p333]**

5.199 True. [I. p2265]

5.200 False. They are commonly accidental due to impurities. **[B. p358]**

Reference Texts

Note: References in the answers sections are given in the format: **[F. p294]**. This indicates, for example, that the topic relating to that particular MCQ may be found on page 294 of the text listed at '**F**' below.

A. Kendell RE, Zealley AK, editors. Companion to Psychiatric Studies. 5th ed. London: Churchill Livingstone, 1993.
B. Johnstone EC, Freeman CPL, Zealley AK, editors. Companion to Psychiatric Studies. 6th ed. London: Churchill Livingstone, 1998.
C. Stein G, Wilkinson G, editors. Seminars in General Adult Psychiatry. London: Gaskell, 1998.
D. Healy D. The Anti-depressant Era. Cambridge (MA): Harvard University Press, 1997.
E. Kaplan HI, Sadock BJ. Pocket Handbook of Psychiatric Drug Treatment. Baltimore (MD): Williams and Wilkins, 1993.
F. Kaplan HI, Sadock BJ. Pocket Handbook of Clinical Psychiatry. Baltimore (MD): Williams and Wilkins, 1990.
G. Eysenck M. Simply Psychology. Hove: Psychology Press, 1996.
H. Sims A. Symptoms in the Mind: an Introduction to Descriptive Psychopathology. 2nd ed. London: W. B. Saunders Company Ltd., 1995.
I. Sadock BJ, Sadock VA, editors. Kaplan and Sadock's Comprehensive Textbook of Psychiatry. 7th ed. Philadelphia (PA): Lippincott Williams and Wilkins, 2000.
J. Brown D, Pedder J. Introduction to Psychotherapy: an Outline of Psychodynamic Principles and Practice. 2nd ed. London: Routledge, 1991.
K. Bateman A, Holmes J. Introduction to Psychoanalysis: Contemporary Theory and Practice. London: Routledge, 1995.
L. Marneros A, editor. Late-Onset Mental Disorders: the Potsdam Conference. London: Gaskell 1999.

M. Malhi, GS, Mitchell AJ. Examination Notes in Psychiatry, Basic Sciences: a Postgraduate Text. Oxford: Butterworth-Heinemann, 1999.

N. Butler R, Pitt B, editors. Seminars in Old Age Psychiatry. London: Gaskell 1998.

O. Hawton K, Salkovskis PM, Kirk J, Clark DM, editors. Cognitive Behaviour Therapy for Psychiatric Problems: a Practical Guide. Oxford: Oxford University Press, 1989.

P. Goodman R, Scott S. Child Psychiatry. Oxford: Blackwell Science, 1997.

Q. Hamilton M, editor. Fish's Clinical Psychopathology: Signs and Symptoms in Psychiatry. Revised reprint. Bristol: John Wright and Sons Ltd., 1974.

R. Puri BK, Sklar J. Examination Notes for the MRCPsych Part I. Kent: Butterworths, 1989.

S. Stahl SM. Psychopharmacology of Antipsychotics. London: Martin Dunitz, 1999.

T. Stahl SM. Essential Psychopharmacology: Neuroscientific Basis and Practical Applications. 2nd ed. Cambridge: Cambridge University Press, 2000.

U. Puri BK, Hall AD. Revision Notes in Psychiatry. London: Arnold, 1998.

V. Buckley P, Bird J, Harrison G. Examination Notes in Psychiatry: a Postgraduate Text. 3rd ed. Oxford: Butterworth-Heinemann, 1995.

W. Kalat JW. Biological Psychology. 5th ed. Pacific Grove (CA): Brooks/Cole, 1995.

X. Gelder G, Gath D, Mayou R, Cowen P. Oxford Textbook of Psychiatry. 3rd ed. Oxford: Oxford University Press, 1996.

Y. Stahl SM. Psychopharmacology of Antidepressants. London: Martin Dunitz, 1999.

Z. Silverstone T, Turner P. Drug Treatment in Psychiatry. 5th ed. London: Routledge, 1995.

AA. Hughes P. Dynamic Psychotherapy Explained. Oxford: Radcliffe Medical Press, 1999.

BB. British Medical Association and the Royal Pharmaceutical Society of Great Britain. British National Formulary. Number 31. London: The Pharmaceutical Press, 1996.

CC. Jacob LS. Pharmacology: the National Medical Series for Independent Study. Baltimore (MD): Williams and Wilkins, 1992.

DD. McKenna PJ. Schizophrenia and Related Syndromes. Hove: Psychology Press, 1997.

EE. Atkinson RL, Atkinson RC, Smith EE, Bem DJ. Introduction to Psychology. 11th ed. Orlando (FL): Harcourt Brace, 1993.

FF. Tantam D, Birchwood M. Seminars in Psychology and the Social Sciences. London: Gaskell, 1994.

GG. World Health Organization. The ICD-10 Classification of Mental and Behavioural Disorders: Clinical Descriptions and Diagnostic Guidelines. Geneva: World Health Organization, 1992.

HH. American Psychiatric Association. Diagnostic and Statistical Manual of Mental Disorders Fourth Edition: DSM-IV. Washington (DC): American Psychiatric Association, 1994.

II. King DJ. Seminars in Clinical Psychopharmacology. London: Gaskell, 1995.

JJ. Liebert RM, Liebert LL. Liebert and Spiegler's Personality Strategies and Issues. 8th ed. Pacific Grove (CA): Brooks/Cole, 1998.

KK. Clark DM, Fairburn CG, editors. Science and Practice of Cognitive Behaviour Therapy. Oxford: Oxford University Press, 1997.

LL. Parkes CM, Stevenson-Hinde J, Marris P, editors. Attachment Across the Life Cycle. London: Routledge, 1991.

MM.Bloch S, Hafner J, Harari E, Szmukler GI. The Family in Clinical Psychiatry. Oxford: Oxford University Press, 1994.

NN. Kaplan HI, Sadock BJ, editors. Comprehensive Textbook of Psychiatry. 6th ed. Baltimore (MD): Williams and Wilkins, 1995.

OO. Bazire S. Psychotropic Drug Directory1998: the Professionals' Pocket Handbook and Aide Memoire. Salisbury: Quay Books, 1998.